You Alone?

One Woman's True Story Of Sensual Awakening

By
Natalie Sommers

© **Copyright [2025]   All rights reserved.**

The contents of this book may not be reproduced, duplicated or transmitted without direct written permission from the author.

Under no circumstances will any legal responsibility or blame be held against the publisher for any reparation, damages, or monetary loss due to the information herein, either directly or indirectly.

Legal Notice:

This book is copyright protected. This is only for personal use. You cannot amend, distribute, sell, use, quote or paraphrase any part or the content within this book without the consent of the author.

Disclaimer Notice:

Please note the information contained within this document is for educational and entertainment purposes only. Every attempt has been made to provide accurate, up to date and reliable complete information. No warranties of any kind are expressed or implied. Readers acknowledge that the author is not engaging in the rendering of legal, financial, medical or professional advice. The content of this book has been derived from various sources. Please consult a licensed professional before attempting any techniques outlined in this book. By reading this document, the reader agrees that under no circumstances is the author responsible for any losses, direct or indirect, which are incurred as a result of the use of information contained within this document, including, but not limited to, —errors, omissions, or inaccuracies.

Table of Contents

Preface..1

Chapter 1 A Gentleman First...3

Chapter 2 How Steamy Novels Are Written.............................38

Chapter 3 Next Level Achieved..81

Chapter 4 Conservative Panties...123

Chapter 5 Like We've Never Experienced..............................154

Chapter 6 Did You Drop From Heaven?..................................197

Chapter 7 Another Crazy Cat Lady..254

Chapter 8 Focus – Lost and Regained......................................299

Chapter 9 It's Getting Hard To Type..356

Chapter 10 Do We Have to Wait Any Longer?......................402

Chapter 11 Are You Sure You're Ready?................................456

Chapter 12 Last Minute Cancellation.......................................512

Chapter 13 I Want You NOW..575

Preface

On these pages, you'll find the word-for-word text message thread between me and a man I met on a dating app one summer. It became a relationship that changed my life. He was someone who turned my life around at the exact right moment and in the exact way I needed.

A few months before I met Nic, my then-husband moved several states away from me and my children without notice. Not only did he move away, but he also took all of our belongings with him. He even changed our address without telling me.

The betrayal, loss, and fear I felt after that incident was almost too much to bear. I was a shell of my former self. Never before have I felt such a deep and visceral sense of hurt and shock as I did then.

A few months after the crippling betrayal, I moved into my own apartment and started my life over.

Once the divorce was in motion, I began scrolling on a dating app. The excitement of having a list of available men was enthralling. I was in search of a passion that I had been dreaming about for years – even while married to my husband.

I knew I wasn't looking for a boyfriend or, most certainly, a new husband. I had another agenda. Although, I wasn't sure how to frame my agenda or explain it to someone else.

I also knew I didn't want a one-night stand or to sleep around with a bunch of men.

None of that felt right to me.

Then along came Nic.

He was like no one I had ever met. He was truly enthralled with me and I was with him. We matched on so many levels but yet came from vastly different backgrounds.

You'll read throughout the book that Nic often seemed to know just what to say to me and even *when* to say it.

As the saying goes, people come into your life for a reason, a season, or a lifetime. Nic and I found each other for a mutually beneficial reason, in a particularly traumatic season and for a lifetime.

Note: Although all the events and dialogue in this book are true to real life, all names and locations have been changed to protect privacy.

Chapter 1
A Gentleman First

> Sat 22 July

1:20 am

> Good evening!

> Hi there Nic

> How are you Beautiful ?

> Natalie!

> Hi there. I'm good but I'm pooped. Going to bed now. Chat tomorrow?

> Sure. Sounds good. Have a blast tomorrow!

> Sat 22 July

> How was your day beautiful?

3:22 pm

> Good thanks. And yours?

> Just got home from kayaking lots of fun found like 50 golf balls

> Nice. Do you golf?

I just got clubs on Father's Day. I played 12 years of Travel Hockey so I'm probably really good at it just haven't yet!

Do you golf?

5:27 pm

> No I don't. My fave NHL team growing up was the Hartford Whalers 😆

The fucking Whalers Babe we have got to talk. I'm messing.

6:19 pm

> Ha!

Who even played for the Whalers?

6:23 pm

> Let me tell you my deal. There is a chance I got on this app slightly too soon. I've been separated since April. I have two 17 year olds who fend for themselves most of the time. But at the moment I have my 8 year old full time. My ex lives in Colorado. We're trying to figure out right now where my little one will live this year. (He wants to be in Colorado).

> So I figured I could date at that time. I'm sorry to be weird like this.
> Who played for the Whalers?
> Sylvain Turgeon
> Gordie Howe
> Ron Francis.

> What I'm trying to say is I'd like to keep chatting and see if we want to meet, it just may be tricky to actually meet in person because I'd need someone to watch my little guy 😊.

< Babe Gordi did not play while you were watching. I'm totally non judgemental with open communication. 17 year olds are they twins? I have twins! Not weird at all it's life.

6:34 pm

> Yes they are twins! Fraternal. I know Gordie was not when I watched them 😛 how old are your twins? Mine are boys.
> And Thanks for understanding.

< 14 year old Boy /Girl
< So I have potent baby batter so we have to be careful 😢 🤣 😋 😉

6:37 pm

> Oh my goodness! No more babies!

Ok but I like practice 😢 🤣

6:46 pm

Ok easy Tiger 😆

I'm just being honest with you.
Communication is key Babe
Would you move to Colorado?

6:52 pm

That's another thing. Great question. Most likely I'd move to Colorado in a year or two. The twins graduate in one year. So it'd be after that.
I totally appreciate your honesty!

My life is kind of crazy right now. So much change. Are you more settled than me?

Well I won't lie, I'll always treat you with respect, I don't want a wife again. I'm searching for some fun, responsible, casual, safe.

6:57pm

I like that.
I definitely am not looking for a new husband.

I don't like this app for its delays. It's hard to get to know someone in real time. If you are comfortable 5559832271.
I'm not pushing an agenda so I get it if you are not comfortable.

7:06 pm

I can call you as soon as I can.
I'm not sure when exactly at the moment. There's no privacy in my place if I'm not alone.

I meant for text TBH. I'm not wanting a phone call 🙈 sorry I shoulda been more clear lol.

7:14 pm

That's good. I got ya. Text is good. I'll text you now.

7:15 pm

Hey. It's Natalie

Hey there Beautiful!

What do you do for work? I've been meaning to ask you?

> I write marketing materials for businesses. And you do something culinary?

I was a Chef for 10 years and now a General Manager for the last 7 years.

> Very cool.

Do you like to cook?

> Ummmm….I do like it. But I don't take time to do it often.

Maybe I can show you the basics.

> That would be amazing actually.

What kind of food do you like? Cuisine, meals.

> I don't love meat unless its prepared really well (so I usually don't make it LOL). I like Indian, Italian, Mediterranean.
>
> Do you have a specialty?

> Rack of lamb is my fave. But TBH I'm a simple man and use basic cooking techniques to bring out the bold natural flavor.
>
> I love Indian. Tell me your Indian spot.

< I don't even know how to tell you where they are. I've been to two around here. I've lived here for six years only. Before that I lived in Colorado for two years.

> Ok I'll find a good one for our first date geez. Thought you had a spot 🙂 😉

< Ugh I'm lame. Sorry 😬

> I like lame. Usually means there's something better hiding 🤭

> Sorry too far
> I don't go out much either. 🤷‍♂️

< It'll be fun. Just not sure yet when that can happen. I'll figure it out.

> I feel like I can hear your personality in your writing. I love that.

Hey now I'm not looking for a date tomorrow again I have no agenda here. I am flirting with you and getting to know you. Whatever happens happens. Low pressure positive vibes only.

> YES!

I write from my mind and heart. I don't sugar coat. I have a sharp tongue. HR hates me. I want fun and laughter.

> I love that! You're like the Michael Scott to the Toby.

Who?

> The Office reference. My fave show.

Wow. Funny I don't watch The Office BUT do you know who Ricky Gervais is? Creator of The Office

> Absolutely.

I should write jokes for him that's how deep and dark and layered I can get. So if I say something crazy it's always meant to be funny. Never insulting.
My kids tell me to put it back in my pocket all the time because of some of the stuff I say.

> I love it. I live to laugh.

Oh well put your seatbelt on and enjoy the ride

> I'm here for it.

Don't be getting me all Hot and bothered.

> Same

Well it is my job isn't it?

>

My Queen.

A true gentleman.

Yes my mom raised me right. Don't get me wrong I have another side 🤷‍♂️

I see both sides, don't worry.
I have to get going now. Talk more soon?

Ok

I know you older ladies go to bed early but I'm up if you want to chat 😉 😊 🤪 😬

Hey now

Don't get your panties in a bunch I'm flirting.
I like Cougars.
More fun 🤩 😊

Do you like younger guys?

Never thought of it before but now I do.

I'm sure it will be fun don't worry.

I agree.

Tell me more about you.

Hmmmmm.

Don't know where to begin?

I won't judge anything you say. I'm an open book if you want to go question for question I will.

Ok.
I was a teacher for many years and hated it most of that time.

> What's that song I'm hot for teacher?

> Van Halen right?

< I think so.
< What bands do you listen to?

> Lol oh Babe. We won't align on music. But it's ok. I like everything except country and derogatory Rap. I love Van Halen, Led Zeppelin, Greta van Fleet, Tom Petty But my heart is with UK House music.
>
> Don't be judgy I'm still fun?

< I like those but what the heck is the house music?

< Sorry, no judgement. Only curiosity.

> I can tell you are reserved so you won't even like it so I'm not even going to share.

< Ha!
< No problem.
< Respect.

> It's party boy music lol.

> Huh. Ok. Like *NSYNC?

> Fuck sakes no.

> Oops. My bad.

> Lol,
> What's your JAM.

> I'm all over the place. I love Classic Rock, Pop, new stuff. Jazz. The only music I really don't love is country.

> I forget. Do you drink?

> You can't forget info that you haven't heard 😁

> Yes.
>
> Do you?

> Sometimes it's on the profile dude.

> I do a little.

> Not every week.

> What's your go to drink?

Well I'm a whiskey drinker. But I love a gold ole fashioned. I love wine bars tho.

> Old fashion was my dad's favorite
>
> This summer I discovered vodka and pink lemonade. Love it.

Wait til you discover Vodka pink lemonade and cougar bait That's Money!! 😋

> Tell me more
>
> ?

> Don't make me type it, I'm blushing. I talk a lot of shit but am shy too ya know.

< Ok. But I still don't know what that drink is….

> You are so silly did you not read it

> Babe you are a Cougar.
>
> I am = bait.

< Oh yeahhhh.
<
< Got it.
<
< Oh boy.

< That's what I thought. For real.

> Sure it is.

< I don't know much about drinks so I thought it was a drink I hadn't heard of 😄

> I may be a bit much for you just saying.

> I think that's very possible

It doesn't turn me off but I also don't want to disappoint you.

> That couldn't disappoint me. I'm worried about it being the other way around. You ok explaining jokes now and then?

I'll explain anything you don't get. If I say something way off please speak up I don't want to ever offend.

> That's a deal. I don't get offended easily.
>
> I'm sort of proper but not uptight.
>
> I'm from Connecticut. If that explains anything.

I don't understand the Connecticut link but I think you may just need to relax and open up a little to have some fun.

> You are so right.
>
> Dead on.

I know I can read through the lines pretty good.

> Yes, I felt that.

> Do I have permission to ask questions?

Sure. Thanks for asking that. See that's the gentleman side. I have a little more time before my youngest comes home.

> Please remember I am a gentleman first.

Yes.

> Do you have a sensual side, sexual, cravings?

I think so.

If I'm understanding you right.

> You're more educated than me so I'm sure you're reading it right

😌
Ok then.

I haven't had great sex in a long time.

> What do you consider great sex?

> That one will need some thoughts on my part.
>
> I think I'd say.
>
> Equally passionate on both parts.
>
> Like movie sex

Well don't be so reserved damnit.

> Hee hee!

Relax it's just me. I'm just trying to get to know you.

> I'm good and relaxed.

> I have to really like the person and feel very safe.

> I would never want to make love to you unless we connect. You are a woman not a pin cushion.

Awesome use of metaphor.

Yes. Thanks. Agree.

> Like I said I talk shit and have fantasies but I am shy

Perfect combo.

> I'm more submissive until I'm told to do otherwise I don't even spank because to me it's abuse I will if asked. I know I'm weird.

Yes abuse comes to mind.

Spanking is way outside my comfort zone 😄

And not that appealing sounding.

> Have you read 50 Shades?

No I haven't. Have you?

No. I just chalk you up to that kind of steamy sex kinda chic.

Hmmm I'm ok with that. All my friends have read it.

I didn't want to read it when it came out bc I knew I'd get too hot and have nothing to do with that energy.

Do you have ANY fantasies?

I'm not sure.

I have to say good night soon. Little guy is coming home soon.

Well shit maybe you could read it to me in bed since I don't like to read and then you will know what to do with the energy 🤣🤣😋👀😈

That may work. Damn where's the blushing emoji when you need it.

Don't blush. Embrace maybe I can open your mind up so you can enjoy life in a different way 🤷‍♂️

Sounds amazing. I just have to be ready for it.

> Well let me know when you are. I'm not talking about ducking you either. I can very well get you going just via text. You just need to let me know if that's something you would enjoy. I'm not going to push the topic but I think you need to live a little.

You are right. But not ready for text stuff. But thanks 💕

> No worries.
>
> I think you are amazing.
>
> Have a great night.
>
> Chat soon.

Omg thanks! You're pretty awesome too.

Night.

> Sweet dreams Babe.

Mon, 24 Jul

10:36 am

Mon, 24 Jul

10:15 pm

WYD

Hanging with my little guy. How about you?

Relaxing in my chair.

Have a nice night 🥴 wish I could talk.

Hey there no worries. Whenever you are ready or can.

Thank you 💕 your vibe is so appealing.

To be clear we are very different but I feel your vibe intriguing. Just call it like I see it.

Yes we are very different. I'm liking that.

You know where to find me 🥴

Tue, 25 Jul

2:54 pm

WYD

> In Cleveland. Sitting in a pizza place working while my son is at a music camp for the day.

What are you working on?

> I'm writing an outline for a video for a YouTube creator.

Oh I thought you were writing a hot steamy novel 🤣

> Ha!!!

About us 😁

> Ha ha! Awww...

C'mon live a little.

> I know I know.
>
> Girls gotta put food on the table though.

> Between my sensual mind and your creative writing we could make a whole series.

That's true. If we could get through it 😊

> That would be part of the process and actually fun to withhold until certain parts of the book / chapter / series 😉

You are right about that.

> Do we need a title? 🤭

Probably.

> 50 Shades of Oh wait. Already taken.

4:45 pm

> You thinking of me?

I have been. How'd you know? 😊

The weather.

The weather?

I heard some thunder

And lightning

I'll hold the umbrella so our notebook doesn't get wet.

You like it quit laughing.

You're right. Guilty.

I can't really tell.

You can't?

Wed, 26 Jul

8:48 pm

WYD

Hanging with the little guy. How about you?

Enjoying these storms thinking of you

You are too cute.

I've been trying to tell you this

😂 💕 You make me laugh.

That's my job isn't it?

Yes!! You understand the assignment

Then let me do my job! 👀 🤣 🥴 🥴
👄

> I am!
>
> Aren't I?

You're getting better.

When are we going for ice cream?

> That's a very good question.
>
> I'm really not sure because I have my 8 year old with me most of the time right now.
>
> I'm 90% sure that when school starts that won't be the case.

Babe low pressure I'm just trying to keep your flame lit 🔥 until you have some alone time. Relax.

> You are doing an amazing job of keeping that flame lit.
>
> Oh boy.

I like to poke fire a little bit.

> Hee hee
>
> How far does thunder sound? Like if I hear Thunder, do you hear the same?

> I feel you Babe.

 I love how you text. It kills me.

Nic sends me two pictures of brightly colored fish in a purple-ish glowing aquarium. The fish and coral look iridescent in the darkness of the night-lit background.

> I'm killing you what?

Your texting kills me. I love it.

> In a good way right.

YES!!

I wanna hear it again

What's with the coral?

Will you be my mermaid?
That's hot just go with it.

Yes. But I'm keeping my legs. Sorry.

I want your legs too don't worry.

> That's good 😛
>
> I gotta go hang with my boy. Have a cozy night.
>
> Did you just hear that thunder?

I'll be up if you want to let some more flirts out.

> Ok. 😃 😄

The thunder sound was me grumbling because you have to hang up.

>

K bye.

> Ok bye.

You mean chat soon but ok.

> Yes.

Thur, 27 Jul

8:41 am

Morning

Hey

How'd you sleep

Better than usual. Thanks. And you?

Send me a pic please.

Not right now.

Promise.

Sure. Yes.

To be clear, I'm not asking for a nude pic

> No worries there. That's not my thing 🤣

I know. I just want to make sure you didn't think I was trying to cross a line.

> I appreciate that. Thank you.

I just think you are pretty and I like seeing who I'm talking to and to feel the moment 🤷‍♀️

> Awwww. Thank you. I've been actually thinking about sending you one just in the past day or so. It's like you can read my mind. It's very freaky.

Oh I can be freaky but you aren't ready 🤣 👀 😗

> That's totally true.

I know it's in you I'll be patient.

> I don't think I'll be as freaky as you are hoping for.

I think you are wrong. I don't need a freak.

> Well, that's good to hear.

Like when I say I can be a freak I don't mean whips and chains. I'm not into any of that.

> Oh phew!

It's hard for me to even spank a woman during sex because it reminds me of violence. Yes I have a naughty mind and fantasies but nothing too weird.

> Oh that's right I remember you said that before.

See I'm not that bad I just talk shit lol.

> Ok good 😆

> Geez I'm just trying to get you to relax and open up your mind a little.
>
> I think you need your hair played with or pulled lol.

Probably. But not pulled mister. Ouch.

> Yes ma'am.

> Can I kiss the back of your neck?

Melting.

> You smell so good

Thur, 27 Jul

3:33 pm

I'm going to look cute tomorrow because I'm going to a concert. I'll make sure I get a pic for you.

> Honestly I like unfiltered and natural but I'll take what I can get.

  I just want to make sure to look cute for you.

> We would not be talking if I wasn't attracted to you.

Awwww.

> When I ask for a pic it's to be in the moment with you. Not you dolled up at a concert. I get if you are uncomfortable or not used to this. But I want to see that smile like yesterday.

Oh, I get it. I see what you're saying. That's awesome. I'll try to do that at some point.

> Geez relax I'm not asking you to shoot a porn Yet! 🤭

😂 The son is getting in the car in a minute, so I can't text.

> Oh are we hiding me 🤭
> Kinda hot.

Yes now shhhhh.

> Yes ma'am.

Chapter 2
How Steamy Novels Are Written

Fri, 28 Jul

8:00 am

GM

GM

WYD

I'm working on content for that YouTube channel. It's super fun and exciting. Then I go to The Velvet Tango Room to watch my boy perform!

It's that new writing gig I got.

What if I want to be the new gig you got someday 😆

I freakin love your texts 😆

❤️ 🤨 Are you still hiding me 🤣

I hate to tell you this, but I gotta go shower now

> Christ sakes.

Hee hee.

> Perfect pic opportunity 👀

💕

I'm only separated dude

Divorce not final yet.

> Do you still love him?

Nope. Only as a partner to raise our kids with.

> Is the divorce paperwork a moral obligation for you not to have fun via text?
>
> Asking for a friend.

> No. I think we're having fun via text now right? Or do you mean something else?

I don't understand why you said you are only separated.

> Oh because I'm hiding you from my kids.

Oh ok.

> I know they don't want me to date.

I hear you on this.

I'll play along.

But it better be worth the wait.

Totally flirting 👆

They call it a sneaky link for a reason.

> What's that?

Side piece that you are hiding

> Haaa!
>
> I'm mostly waiting for my ex to go back to Colorado with my little one.

> Be spontaneous and send me a damn pic. 😜 live for once in your life like you are free.

> 😛I will. But need to shower now.

> 🙂I'm only wanting you to laugh and have fun.

> I know. 🙏

> And don't be thinking of me in the shower I know you ladies can get carried away in there.

> 😂 😂

>

> Have an amazing day.

>

> Lol.

> You make that sound like goodbye geez

> Chat soon.

> Sorry Ok!

Fri, 28 July

8:31 pm

I send Nic a selfie of me looking in the bathroom mirror. I'm wearing a blue tank top and have only a partial smile. My phone is partially in the way of my face. I hate doing this but I know he'll love it. So here I am.

> Look at you beautiful! How are you?
> Almost a smile too.
> How was your day?

> It was good. My son had an amazing performance in Cleveland. He made it into the Cleveland Jazz festival. I've just been doing work for a few hours and stopped to take a break and think about you.

> Is that you now? Or earlier?

> Just now.

Thank you I'm very excited that you sent me a pic ♥

I know it's not your thing.

I send Nic a picture of a stemless wine glass partly filled with white wine perched on my balcony railing with the sun setting behind it in the distance.

You look great tho.

Oh mommy juice.

Yes.

On my balcony.

> Mmmmm.
>
> What have you been thinking about me?

Thanks for the yummy compliments.

> I just call it like I see it.

I can't wait to hang out. I think we're gonna have fun.

> Yeah but you need to relax and just have fun.

I think I'll be able to for the most part.

> I'll help you.

I know.

I seriously think this is how steamy novels are written.

> Maybe we are creating one and we don't even know it.

I know right? Although I've been deleting all our texts sadly.

> Wow no trace at all eh?

> No, and I'm not happy about it.

Am I that weird that you have to hide me .

> Hell no.

Why do you delete them?

Just asking.

> It's a momma guilt thing.

Ok I get it.

I'll have the copyright then.

> I just want you for me.

Be careful what you ask for.

>

I don't think you are ready for all of this yet.

Take another sip.

I'm having a cocky too so relax.

Cocktail.

Cocky 🤷‍♂️🙍‍♀️

> Laughing out loud on my balcony alone Cocky 😁

You're not alone I'm just not allowed to be there, Maybe I can sneak on the deck for a kiss.

> I wish but it's on the second floor. You'd need a ladder.

Wow short jokes ouch.

> I'm probably giving my 8 year old son to my ex for the school year in two weeks and may need some hugs.

I'm always down for hugs. Cuddling is the best. It doesn't always have to be about sex even tho I may come off as a horn ball.

> 😊
> I may also get a kitten when Will leaves So then I'll be the old maid with cats.

Great another crazy cat lady

> Goals

Not commenting

> Ha,
>
> I left you speechless.
>
> Do you live with your kids part time?

Typically every other weekend.

Your pic left me speechless

>

I was shocked.

> That's what I was going for,
>
> Shock value and that raw unfiltered look.

Next time move the damn phone so I can see all of your beautiful face.

> Ooops. Ok.

No oops. Baby steps. I dig it Babe.

When's the last time you cuddled someone?

That is the most phenomenal question I've been asked in ages.

I don't even know how long it's been

So I'm going to be the first in a long time

Yep.

Pretty soon I have to get back to the work I was doing. You were my break.

Break with mommy juice I'll take it.

Tell me it's super fun being single and just having flirty casual dates with girls.

If you want to chat I'll be here and I'm always down for more smiley pics.

I don't casual date. I don't have a lot of money after the divorce so I don't get to go out much. I want to wine and dine you but a picnic is probably more so in your near future. I haven't dated anyone since March and she was for 9 months. Being honest with you.

I love the honesty. Very sexy.

Take me for who I am and make you feel.

Yes!

And I love picnics.

What real woman doesn't?

Get back to the grind babe I'll be here.

Got it. Thanks for giving me an awesome break!

Oh you will be doing a working break next time

If you don't mind

Anyways go or I'll flirt your ear off.

Fri, 28 Jul

10:41 pm

Ma'am!

> Yeeeessss....

I'm thinking of you.

>

WYD I'm whispering.

> Still working (I'm whispering also).

Let me work with you.

> I'm writing a YouTube script about menopause

It's hot in here eh.

Line one.

Write it down.

> Ha!!!!!

Lol.

> Ok.
> LOL.

> You better be smiling.
>
> I'll leave you be as you are too dang cute.

> I am.
>
> Thank you. You make me laugh

> I want you to giggle too tho.

> You've been making me giggle every day.

> What's after giggling and laughing?
>
> Whatever it is I want that.

> I love how you put things. ♥

> Blunt,
>
> Raw,
>
> Uncut.

> Also witty and funny.

> Power couple in the making.

> 😆

> What?
> 🤣 Can't a guy fucking dream about cougars being tamed in the wild,
> Sorry I swear don't take it to heart.

> LOL RN.

> Second floor so I have to throw pebbles at your window to get your attention is that what I read?

> Exactly.

> Once I get your attention how will I know how I can keep it?

> Such a great question. Not sure I have the answer.
> You're keeping it so far that's for sure.

> Am I out-writing the writer?
> I think I should be a writer.

> You totally could be.

I missed my calling.

> I'm in my second career. Just sayin.

Porn didn't work out eh!
kidding.

> Ha!!!!
> Actually teaching children didn't work out.

You're still young, you can teach me. I'm younger.

> I see where you're going with this.

Whoa I have no agenda. I'm just flirting.

Don't take that the wrong way?

> I don't take you the wrong way. At least I think I don't. No worries.

I was actually going to admit I missed my calling to be a phone sex operator.

Hot steamy cat women can do it.

> There's got to be a dad bod hot steamy market for women.

I'm on board.

> How can I make it in front of the masses and make it a business tho?

Hmmmmm.

> Speechless on business or just want me for yourself
>
> I'm ok with either answer.

The business idea

> If I could make a lot of women feel the way I make you feel how powerful is that?

Unreal. Off the charts.

> I want that.
>
> I like what we do for each other.

Same

It's been so wild and fun chatting with you.

> We are opposites right?

> WDY mean?

> You are reserved like the 1913 room at the Amway Grand.
> I'm a loose cannon trying to get you to have fun.

> That sounds about right.

> If you know a way to get that business model off the ground I'm all ears

> I'll brainstorm. It's a tough one though.

> I know nothing about the space or what platform to use. I'm not tech savvy.
> But I can fantasize like the best of em

> Yes you can 😄

> And I have a feeling you can too.

> Ummmmm.

> It's ok.
>
> You don't have to blush nor answer.

> Thank you. You are very understanding. For real.

> I do seek for you to be more open day by day tho. No rush but I crave you to be open and relaxed. I'm not here to harm or anything. I just want to have fun.

> Well I sense that is happening.
>
> The open part not the harm part.

> Tell me a secret.
>
> Doesn't have to be weird.

> Thinking.
>
> I can't think of one RN.
>
> You tell me one.

> I was a cheerleader in my senior year.

> Ummmm. Was there a pretty girl on the team you were trying to woo??
>
> But really that's amazing.

> No. A male classmate wanted to join and even though boys were allowed to do everything the girls could do, the Athletic Director said NO. So being anti authority 7 of us stood with him and joined

> That's absolutely amazing.

It was never heard of till 2000.

Not in my school.

> Ground breaker.
>
> Impressive.

I hated the who rah cheering part.

> Hopefully the girls loved having you guys

I loved tossing the girls and the liberty pose.

To be there and protect them from falling was a rush.

> Wow.
>
> So cool.

No I never dated or slept with any of em. I'm sure you may think that's where I was going but no.

> You caught me. That is seriously a cool story though.

Do you do yoga?

> Holy hell I just wrote the word yoga when you texted that.
>
> Wait I'll show you.

I send Nic a screenshot of a Google Doc with a list of words written in a column: aerobic exercise, yoga, meditation.

> And yes I do!
>
> But I want to do it more often.

> I want to do couples yoga.
>
> Like sexy hot balancing each other yoga.
>
> Do you know what I'm talking about?

> I've seen it on Instagram I think
> Do you do yoga then ?

> I have. I am no good but I liked it.
>
> It has to be the right setting for me. I want to learn the moves so when they are called out I know what the fuck to do instead of feeling like a creep staring at the female instructor for the next move 👀 🤭

> Ha! I always look at the instructor! No shame. Where have you gone to practice? Any studio around here?

No. TBH It was with my girlfriend in New Mexico. It's been a minute. I'll need to stretch.

> Me too.
>
> Is she the one from March? The 9 month one?

No she was 2 years ago in New Mexico. March was here in Ohio.

> Ahh. Ok.

New Mexico was 24. Ohio was 51.

Age isn't a thing for me. I'm looking for connection.

> Lucky for me 😒
>
> I'm looking for connection too but I'm not sure it's in the same way as you.
>
> I just ended a 20+ year marriage.

What do you crave Natalie? What is it? Maybe I'm ok with what you say and you think I only want totally more.

This is not the time to be shy or hesitate this is communication.

> I crave someone to go out with/hangout with once in a while. Someone to chat like this with. Someone who is ok if we don't talk every day or see each other every week. Someone who is ok not meeting my kids.

I don't want or need to meet your kids. I can't give you a 7 day relationship as I have a career, kid obligations and I like some me time too. I can I think provide what you are looking for if I'm reading this right. And no it doesn't mean sex.

If I'm off please align me with your ideas.

> You are so f'ing refreshing and honest and straightforward. I'm freaking out over here.
>
> It sounds like you get me.

I have only been open and honest in my needs and wants and if you do the same we can decide if we are looking for the same thing. If not then we are wasting time.

> Totally agree.

So from now on I don't want hesitation when I ask for a picture. And from now on what do you want? I'm not talking about stopping in the middle of a speech to take a selfie. I'm flirting remember.

> I just really take a bad picture 😞

I don't even want a good one. That's staged.

I think you are beautiful and amazing or we wouldn't be talking. I crave a side of you that you are trying to open up about.

> Oh my. Gulp. Amazing text again.
> I got to pick up my kid from work in a minute.

As you freshen up to leave it's perfect time for a pic 😉 😘

I send Nic another selfie from my couch. I'm wearing a blue loose fitting shirt and giving the camera a smirky smile. I hope he likes it.

OMG look at you.

> This is me not freshened up.

> Smirking and shit.

>> This is work from home played with my hair all day me.
>>
>> Hee hee.
>>
>> Love texting you. So much.

> I want to play with that hair.
>
> So not fair.

>> Hee 😆.
>>
>> My hair is a whole situation.

> I'll own all of the situation if you play your cards right.
>
> Yup I said it.

>> LOL!!!
>>
>> Cracking me up.

> Of course with your permission
>
> I'd never even think of it

>> Of course. You are a gentleman first.

> Don't bring the Viking out of me.

> Ha!

You like my beard don't you.

> Yes.

> I'm not used to a beard though.

They tickle

Added touch.

> I bet.

No FEE.

> Ha.

You can run your fingers through it and tell me how soft it is.

> Mmmmmm.

I'm getting a few gray hairs but I've embraced them.

That's a good attitude It looks distinguished on a man anyway.

Plus I'm trying to fit in with the older ladies. It's where I belong with a sophisticated one that knows how to write well and goes after her.....

LLLLLLOOOOOOLLLLLL

LAUGHING SO HARD.

Fill in the blank,

Cmon.

Umm.

Stallion, dream, favorite cookies .

Desires???

I like all those.

Mmmmm tell me more.

We knew each other in a former life.

> I bet if you heard me talk right now I could make you wet 🤷‍♂️

Melting.

You are almost too much for me.

> The floor is lava you figure it out.
>
> Not too much maybe it's what you desire.
>
> Your words not mine.

Now I'm all hot and bothered.

How do you do this?

> It's what you desire, so it's what I do.

I'm going to be so embarrassed when we finally meet 😊.

> Why?

I don't know.

It's easier to text maybe.

> You have me melting and honestly hard AF just talking to you. Sorry I'm just being honest.
>
> I'm vulnerable too.

> Oh my again.
>
> No need to apologize.
>
> I'm sorry I need to go now.

When can we chat again?

> In a few days. How does that sound?
>
> I gotta focus on my little one this wknd .

I don't have a choice do I. It's what I signed up for. It's what you desire. Question is can you wait til Monday? Good luck.

> You have had me laughing all night. Thank you
>
> Night night.

So Monday?
And if you message sooner than that you lost your bet.

> You're on.
>
> We'll see what happens…

I'm already throwing boulders at your window.

> You CRACK me up!! I love it.

You already lost WTAF

> Hahaha.

Don't do this to us

Just hide me and chat when you can. I can't wait that long. There I said it.

Good night

Sat, 29 Jul

1:51 am

You awake?

Sun, 30 Jul

12:58 pm

> Thinking of you today even though I can't chat…

It's before Monday. You have lost the bet. Sorry.

> 😞

I'm golfing so you're off the hook now

> Oooh have fun! Get a lot of strikes!

Sun, 30 Jul

7:17 pm

That's bowling silly.

> I was just thinking about you.

Tell me.

> I just can't wait to see you in person.
> I'm not sure you are real.

You already broke your own rule Babe.

> Shit.
> I was trying really hard.

This was your rule.

> I know.

> Can you share a pic?

I send Nic an awkward-looking selfie. I'm wearing a rust-colored T-shirt and reading glasses. My hair is curly and unruly, and I'm half-smiling.

> Look at you. Brave and all. Look at that smile.

So so brave.
This is like the fifth one I took.

> It's ok. It's not easy.
> I'm taking you out of your zone. I get it.
> But it's amazing.
> Am I wrong?

Nope.

> Should I keep going or no. I don't want you to do anything that makes you uncomfortable.

Keep going how?

> Taking you out of your comfort zone silly.

I think it's too uncomfortable.

> I'm not talking about banging you or sending nudes I'm just flirting relax.

Ok then.

> I appreciate you sending me a pic more than you know. I know you are not comfortable. I'm not trying to make you feel uncomfortable, I'm trying to get you to have fun and explore.
> I would rather dry hump you like we are 16 than fuck. Please understand this.

Why is that?

> It's not about sex with me even tho you may think I'm pushing that. I'd rather touch you and make you wet than to penetrate you.

> Ok But I'm still wondering why you have that preference?

Ok I'm in all honesty lol.

I've been drinking all day and sun burnt AF. Lol.

It may be safer if we have clothes on

> Hmmmm.
>
> I just can't wait to meet you.

Are you sidestepping that I'm trying to be safe?

> Safe is important but safe from what?

I'll gladly make love to you and touch you all of the ways. But I was trying to be respectful.

> You are respectful. It's amazing.
>
> And I really appreciate that.

Safe also not trying to have more kids.

> Yes! So true.
>
> 3 is my max.
>
> My little guy is leaving me in a few weeks .

I know that's tough. I'm sorry.

Thanks

I'm not trying to replace him but I can be your lil guy just in a different way.

Thank you ❤️

I am very surprised you broke your own rule. I even wanted to text you this AM and said no because I thought you needed a break from me.

I did want a break. It was fun to miss you and think about you. I was becoming VERY hot and bothered thinking about you before and needed to cool down. That, and hang out with my kids.

I didn't mean a literal break. We are parents and kids need us. I recognize this but also am trying to flirt and make it about us. And our adventure.

You are an expert at flirting.
Just texting you has been driving me crazy.

Just imagine if we had skin to skin contact and I could say this to your face.

Melting again. I'm a puddle.

> Do you have sexual desires when I chat with you?

YEP!!!

> You can share them if you want. If not I completely understand.

I'm not going to say too much but basically it's as if you walked into this room right now you could have me immediately.

> Do you mind if I take over gently?

I'm going out with Will right now though

You have magic powers I'm convinced.

> Awe have fun
>
> He's lucky to have you right now. Probably saved you from a lot of sweating and deep breathing for sure.

Heee heee

Thanks

I'll wait my turn. It will feel so much better.

But I need you to relax.

In time I will.

I want you to get the full experience but you have to just relax and take in the moments.

Yes.

It's just me here right?

Right.

So every time you don't relax it feels like you don't trust me

I'm not wanting harm. I want for you the complete opposite.

I know. It's just that you're still like a stranger. We haven't even met.

That will and should be the fun of this. I ultimately want you to TRUST me and I want to take you somewhere you never have been. Psychologically and or physically. I won't push the second one. But just take it in and tell me if you are ok with it.

Ok.

Well no I actually wanted feedback I don't want this to be Nic's fantasy.

I trust you to a very large extent considering we haven't met.

I feel like I've known you my whole life.

Or in another life 😁

I'm the voice in your head. I'm the naughty one. I mean no harm. I just want you to enjoy life a little.

I LOVE THAT.

I do feel safe with you but it's a little scary. Just a little.

Trust me I know. I'm a stranger. And yes this whole thing can be taken as I'm baiting you into some weird shit. I don't know what else to say or do for you to trust me

I'm glad you get it. But I do trust you.

You've been incredibly sexy but also respectful and funny 😊

> Can I just be real honest.
>
> It's almost like something I saw today.

< K

> K?

< Ok

> I watched Saved By the Bell earlier you've seen it right.

< Yes

> So the episode was Zach (popular kid) was supposed to dance with (unpopular girl). Yes that's me and you and no not specifics on popular and not popular. It's more to me opposites way different people but have cravings and needs too.

< Ok

> I lost you completely.

< Oh so that's your point? That Zach and the girl reminded you of us?

> It's not about them and us.

> It's about two way different people needing a connection.
>
> Wanting to connect.

> We are opposite no doubt.

Sorry. I'm trying to multitask and failing.

I guess we are opposites.

> I do not want you to feel like you are failing that's not what I'm trying to say

Nic, you're not making me feel that way. I'm just doing too much at once.

> You write and publish! I hate reading.
>
> I'm sensual. You are reserved.

Yes.

> That's really the contrast. Not throwing shade. Unless it's shades of gray 👀.

LOL.

I hear ya.

Add to that list you can cook and I can't.

Compromise. Can you make me feel good through flirting back with me 💁

I haven't been? I'm not sure how to do it other than what I was doing.

You can write like a mother fucker probably. Reading is not for me. Let's try this again. Compromise.

I can cook yes.

I will cook for you daily if you keep making me feel good through flirting like you have been.

Yes you also make ME feel important too.

That's the beauty of compromise.

I agree. I'm just not sure I can do all this texting. I gotta get off my phone and take Will out. I'm sorry.

You already have been making me feel good.

Have fun with lil man.

I'm here when you are ready Babe.

I'm glad I've been able to do that. And thanks!

> I wouldn't be keeping this going if I didn't have some benefit too ya know.

Good. I'm glad.

> Maybe I should have been more informative on that. Moving forward I will be open with how you have and make me feel inside.

That's really good. I love your honesty.

It reminds me of Kelly on The Office talking about this guy she liked. 'He says whatever he's thinking. What kind of game is that?'

> Never seen The Office
>
> That's how opposite we are
>
> Go be with little man
>
> I'll be here later. I feel like I'm taking his time.

It's not your fault. But yes. We're going now. Thanks love.

> Love eh.
>
> I'll take that. Mmmmm.

> Mmmmmmm.

Sun, 30 Jul

11:30 pm

> I can't talk now but just wanted to say ♥ been thinking about you ♥.

> Can you text?
>
> Or is that what you mean by talk.
>
> Told you I'm a literal person.

> It means I can't even text

> I'll be up for a while. Maybe say GN if you can

Chapter 3
Next Level Achieved

Mon, 31 Jul

1:11 am

I want you so bad I had to share it with you.

Mee too.

Sorry.

Say more.

Maybe I shouldn't be talking like this.

Its ok.

You sure?

Yes

I want you so bad

You are making me hard. I'm sorry but I said I would be honest on how you made me feel.

> I love our adventure like you called it
>
> I don't think I can wait two weeks for you.

It's not the first time you have me so excited when we text.

> I feel the same way about you.

It doesn't make sense. We don't know each other. Well kinda but not at all really.

> I know.

And I don't just give in to anyone

So why you?

> I feel like we have some crazy strong connection
>
> Opposites attract
>
> Right?

I want to take care of you sexually and mentally. I want to stimulate your mind.

> You already have done both actually.

I want more of both.

> I want you to slide your hand down my panties

Is this permission

> Yes.

You won't even realize what my fingers can do until it's too late
So you're sure?

> Mmmm
> Yes
> Please

I'm gonna stop being a gentleman at some point.

> Please.

My fingers are magical.

> Mmmmm.

But I have to disclose my tongue is where it's at!

> Wet. Very very wet.

Maybe we aren't so opposite. We want the same thing.

> Yes.

Want a fun fact?

> Sorry I'm not writing much
> Yes.

I can breathe through my ears.

> Omg
> I want you so bad RN

Don't apologize for lack of writing. I'm pretty sure I told you I was taking you to another level and to just relax 🦋

> Yes.

Shall I proceed?

> Please.

I love eating pussy especially a wet one.

> I didn't know I could get this wet.

Are you touching yourself?

> Yes.

I want you to.

I'm jealous.

> I wish u were doing it

I will one day if you let me.

> Yes.

> If you could have me RN what would you do to me?

> You'd be sitting on the couch and I'd straddle you
>
> And rub up and down with you inside me

> Look at me when you do that. I want to see your eyes.

> Yes
>
> I'm really hot RN
>
> Wet
>
> Wanting you RN

> You can have me
>
> I am yours
>
> You just have to relax and invite me into your space
>
> Send me a pic not crazy pic don't worry

> I can't right now
>
> Lights r off
>
> I'm too worked up

There is a flash in the camera but I'll respect your shyness. I just want to see how good I've done 😋 😊

You'll see in person.

I want you to just feel me throbbing. I can't even hide it.

I want you in me.

Just the tip

No.
All the way please.

I don't want anymore kids.

I don't think you'll have any with a 50 yo

You can just say leave it in and bury it

Fill you up 🤷

> So you'll go inside me?
>
> With a condom?

I will wear protection if you want me to. I'm clean and no diseases. Just avoiding more kids! 🤷🤷

> Same for me exactly.
>
> I've been with one guy for the past 25 years.

We don't have to have sex. I'm not trying to make you feel that way.

> I think we should.

It would feel amazing.

> Yes.

It want you to feel amazing.

> You have already given me that.

I want to show you more.

> Ok.

Can I ask you a question?

> Y

Are you a freak in the sheets? Like I feel like you are bamboozling me 🤭

> No. You have brought this out in me.
>
> This is not my normal.

Well I'm not forcing anything. I want you to just relax and maybe get fucked. By me duh

> Ok.
>
> You aren't forcing.

I am very good at this so be careful.

> Mmmmm.
>
> You are making me so wet.

You can add pressure to the back of my head whenever you feel necessary.

> Ok

I love making you wet.

> I'm imagining you.

I am so soft down there

The WHOLE tongue

Get it girl.

> Then you'll move up on top of me
>
> Crawl up my body.

Yes ma'am.

> And make me come again.

> Right on my cock
>
> Sorry too far.

No.

> Then do it
>
> I want to feel it
>
> I want to see it too.

Ohhhh myyyyy.

> Shit sorry.

Why apologize?

> I want you so bad.

You did amazing.

I was begging you.

> My mind is in a very naughty place. So I'm apologizing.

< I loved it
< Never done this before.

> Let me just fuck your brains out one time.

< You got it
< This was so fun.

> Did you cum?

< Yes!!

> I love it. 😆
> I like to keep track. It's my job to make you cum.

<

> Seriously.

You texted me tonight right when I was thinking about you.

I want you to destroy my sheets.

Mmmmmm ♥

I'm so hard RN.

I don't know how to help you from here

This is all new.

Nope I just want you to know you have the magic and I appreciate it.

Now I have all this energy since you satisfied me

It feels like noon

I feel like you know me

I have done research

> How?? I'm so curious. What do you know??

I'm messing. But I do know from our convo I want to just remove all negativity from your mood and take over.

> Did you take a class or something? How do you know just what to say?

I wanted you to put your hand on the back of my head
No class, can't it just be what I desire too?

> Sorry about the hand. I was imaging it though.

Don't be sorry silly.

> 😙

I have tomorrow off

> Oh fun.

Ummmm that was more of an invite
Sorry too forward.

> I wish I could take you up on it!! I have Will all day and this week I have to produce twice as much as last week for my work.
>
> What days do you work usually?
>
> Not too forward.

< I'm trying to get you in the mood. I know Will has limited time. Again I'm just flirting.

> ☺ you've succeeded in getting me in the mood. No worries there mister.

< Sweet dreams Babe.

> You too!!
>
> When's your birthday? If you don't mind my asking.

Mon, 31 Jul

5:02 am

< May 1.

> No F'ing way
>
> That is totally crazy
>
> You are not real
>
> I'm sorry I'm freaking out.
>
> You are AI.

As real as they come.

I'm freaking out.

You're not possible.

I am if you just let me.

Mine's the day after yours. I'm going to need proof at some point.

You looked me up online or something. That can't be your birthday.

You're messing with me.

Right!?!

If I give you proof I want to have earned more trust and bond moving forward.

Ok. You'll have deserved it.

Nic sends me a picture of his Ohio license showing the birthday of May 1. I am in total and complete shock at the coincidence of our birthdays being one day apart.

> Omg!!!!!!
> You are so cute

I want you so bad RN

> Mmmmmmm
> Why are we still up?

Is this the only time of day you can sneak me
I was just moving from my chair to bed.
You are the one flirting this time 🤭

I'm innocent.

> I CAN'T BELIEVE OUR BIRTHDAYS ARE SO CLOSE. CAN YOU?
> And I suspected it too.

I mean it is very odd

> So odd

In a good way?????

> YES!!!!!

You're an odd duck. I'm an odd duck.

Yes sir!!

Are you really still up or just wake up?

Still up

You're my odd hot sexy birthday sharing penpal

We should meet somewhere and make out

You need some rest.

You make me laugh so much I love it

But yes

I need to sleep

Night night 😋

I'm so glad I met you.

No wait now I'm up.

Oooooppps....

Have you been drinking wine?

> I've been up for so long now I'm hungry for breakfast
> No wine tonight.

Are you just high on my texts and soooo wet from earlier you couldn't even go to bed?

> EXACTLY

I'm so sorry.

> It's so your fault. 😂

You like it though so I'm not sorry.

> You know me. How do you know me so well?

Send me a pic.

> Ugh. I'll try.

Geez don't sound so bothered.

> I'm sorry I can't
>
> The lights too bright
>
> I did try
>
> Though
>
> I'll try again.

Nic sends me a selfie of him smiling in bed. He has no shirt on and it's very sexy hot.

I want to see you.

Oh my gosh so handsome
And hot.

Hairy not hot.

Both actually.

Nic sends me another pic of his chest, full of chest hair.

For your eyes only.

Oooohhh
Thank you.

I would show you how hard I am but that is way not your style. But just know 😉

Well thank you. You are right.

I still want a pic.

I send Nic a pic. I'm laying on my white pillowcase with my face partially buried in it and my eyes squinting. I'm smiling with my lips closed and my hair is a complete mess.

Was that so bad? ❤️ ❤️ ❤️

I had to squint
😊
The flash is too bright.

Better than me telling you to turn over and bury that face in your pillow while I

> Naughty

Someone has to start the fire
You aren't all innocent and we know this.

> Guilty
> But it's only bc of you
> I never did all this stuff before

Because or for me

> Both

I want you to want to do this. I don't want to feel like I'm leading you on to make you do this.

> Don't worry about that. But thank you for saying that. I physically can't do what makes me uncomfortable.

I just want to be your wildest dreams.
Your fantasy.
Your get away.

> You already achieved that

> Then I want more
>
> What else can I be for you.

Can I just lie here and love that question for a moment.

> Yes but I want an answer or a pic.

No pressure 😄

Since that first pic was a disaster….

> You have me awake and hard AF 5:37 AM so you have already won in my book.

Awwwww but did I win or frustrate you?

> You have never frustrated me ever.

Ok phew.

> Except when you act innocent about sending a pic
>
> Stop being shy it's just me.

> Yes I know. I just want to look good for you.

I only want you to be yourself and that's always good enough for me ALWAYS

>  swoon

I like your natural beauty. We have already gone over this. I'm not wanting a makeup queen with filters.

> Yes I'm so glad ♥
>
> I hardly even wear makeup. But I do like to look cute.

Babe you squinting in the camera is hot AF for me. You are trying and I can see it and how it's tough for you to even snap the pic. Your efforts aren't going unnoticed.

>
> Melting again.

Show me.

> I'm sorry but it's too light. I need darkness so I can sleep. I'm so sorry. I should try to sleep now.

Don't be like that

Give me a goodnight pic so I can go back to bed and continue to dream of you.

Ok hold on.

I send Nic another pic. My face is still against the white pillowcase and I am making a funny smile. My hair is still a mess and the lighting in the room is dim.

I'm gonna make you so wet one day I can't wait.

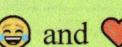 and ♥

Yay!!
You are awesome.

Sweet dreams. I know mine are going to be wet. Chat soon.

LOL

Night night

I can't get you outta my mind. Ok sweet dreams.

Mon, 31 Jul

9:17 am

WYD

Trying to wake up but I'm exhausted

Now Nic sends me a pic of his face and his chest from his bed. Very hot.

Lay with me.

I send Nic a pic of my face with squinting eyes and a closed smile. I'm slowly getting more used to this selfie-sending thing.

> My eyes can't open still

Let them roll back into your head while I touch you softly.

> But I have to get ready to work soon....

Just two minutes.

> Ok.

What do you want me to do to you with those two minutes.

> I don't know. I can't think straight.

Don't be shy now you have control for two minutes.

Just hug me.

You got it. Your wish is my command.

You smell so good.

What will you do on a day off?

Probably have to touch myself at some point you have me all built up 🤷‍♂️ 😜

Oooohhh sounds so good

I have to work as much as I can today. It'll be a little challenging with Will.

Time to shower. Thanks for waking up with me.

Take full advantage of me in the shower please.

I said please 😉

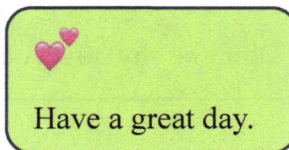

Have a great day.

You too.

I finally muster the courage to send Nic a full length pic. I'm wearing a red well fitting tee shirt, having my glasses on and my hair is very curly. I'm giving him a big smile.

OMG look at you.

That's me trying to work but wanting to send you selfies instead.

Now back to work.

Getting pretty damn good at it

My mind is melting now.

Back to work and never be shy to share more. I like it mmmmmm

Ok

Damn you now I want more

I can't wait to hang out. Not sure when. But excited.

No rush and no hurries but when we do I think we are going to enjoy it.

Mon, 31 Jul

10:00 pm

Miss you.

Miss you too Babe.

I've actually been sort of through hell since April. So the love and attention you've been giving me has been like a natural medicine.

Let me finish strong in July for you then.

You made me happy earlier with that unexpected pic.

I thought that would make you really happy

Can I just say, isn't it weird that our birthdays are one day apart? I'm still giggling over that.

This whole thing is weird. But not like creepy weird.

Right. Just super cool weird.

Crazy to communicate like this and know that we are so opposites but yet want to satisfy each other. If marriages and relationships were just founded on this would more last longer? 🤷

I cannot tell you how you fully 100% read my mind. It is uncanny. I had the same thought today that you just texted. Unreal.

I think that maybe we are just both realists. And we can see things differently than others without judgment or stereotyping.

Please send me another surprise one when you can. And if there is anything I can do for you I'll share or write to you softly. 😊

I just have to say I love just reading your texts and I just feel warm and soft inside. And I mean that mentally and lower down inside 😉

I'll take it as low as you will allow. I'll be patient.

I want you to have that sensation

You get me so riled up. I've got more work I have to finish now 😢

Excuse me Mrs Innocent I'm still hard from this AM pic.

Ooooooopppps

It's not fair.

None of this is fair.

But good job. 😉

Why thank you sir.

Get some work done. But I want some attention soon

> You got it
>
> Deal

I want it. Chat soon.

> I want you in person through.

Not yet. Soon.
Babe I still need to hide remember.

> Yes you do. That's true.

Shhhhhh. Go work and then we can play some.

> Ok.

Pssssstttttt.

> Yeeeesssss
>
> What time were you born?

2:22 pm.

> What a freaking cool time to be born.

I'm a big deal 🤷‍♂️

> I know

I want to see a pic. Please

> Ok I wish I had an even slightly sexy nightgown other than my tee shirt and leggings for you to see.

I don't need the extra. I want to see you silly.

You can show me a nightgown one day when you feel comfortable.

> 👍

> I need to get a nice one first. It's been a minute since I've wanted to wear something cute or sexy for some one.

Do you wear bras?

> Yes.

That's sexy to me.

> Even just the everyday full coverage ones?

I would see enough skin to probably cum like a little school boy.

Sorry too graphic

> Not too graphic. Just funny.
>
> I like metaphors.

> I just finished a whole book on metaphors 😄
>
> Not kidding.

You are silly.

> hee hee

Nic sends me a pic of his blue underwear bulging with his excitement as he sits on his living room chair. in low light. It's very tasteful and hot.

Proof your bra and my brain is enough satisfaction.

Oh my oh my

Ok

I just got really wet.

I will believe you.

Yes you'll have to take my word for it.

Yeah I wasn't asking for a pic of that. Just some pretty lace or loose shirt.

I'm listening to jazz now. I'm so in the mood.

Oooohhhh you're killing me.

I have no lace 😢

Natalie do you think I would get you to go from super conservative to WET pics overnight 🤣 💦 👀

> You practically have.
>
> But not quite.

> Yes I have and I want to again.

> All my kids are still up.

> I won't moan will you ?

> I'm being flirtatious.

>

> Need a fucking ShamWow after we meet the first time
>

>

> Sorry I'm so bad.

I send Nic a picture of just the top of my breasts. My white tee shirt is pulled far down. But I do not show anything more than breast skin.

> Ok so if you haven't already by now know, you are so fucking sexy. They look amazing but I am speechless on your flirting.

Why speechless? And thank you.

> The fact that you are being intentional if it's not for my needs, your needs, hopefully both, but I know it's not comfortable for you. But I have to tell you how sexy you look.

Love your words

I liked doing that for you. And it was fun for me. You're breaking me out of my shell.

> I want you to feel sexy because I think you are sexy.

> You have this raw beauty that doesn't need filters.

Oh my. Swoon.

> You are so fun. Did you like me or did I like you first on the app? I can't remember. Do you?

I hunted you just like I'm doing now

I wanted a nerd crush

> YOU ARE KILLING ME OVER HERE

You like it.

> You are so gd clever. I think I'm the one having the nerd crush.

I'm just wanting to make you happy.

> Success
>
> You so have
>
> You have no idea what brought me to you.

What was it?

I didn't show you my weiner yet.

> Or did I
>
> Kidding.

I'll give you the short version. My husband and I sold our house and moved out in February but instead of finding a new place here he drove our moving truck with all our furniture to our other house in Colorado without telling me. Until he was on his way. It's a long story.

> It's ok. You are ok right? Safe from him? Free to chat here?

Yes

Thanks

He's in town now bc he brought Will back from Colorado. Will was there for the first half of summer.

I am safe from him. Thank you

Now back to us

Just fyi you've had me wet for days now.

> I love that I can take you there
>
> Just my mind
>
> Imagine the touch combined

> I am RN
>
> You are touching me RN.

Where?

> In the wetness.

Have you ever had your pussy spanked or patted when you are wet?

> No.

Sorry it was an odd question.

> I want your
>
> Cock buried deep inside me.

Nic shows me again the effect my words and feelings are having on him with a pic of his bulging blue underwear. I can't deny, it is getting me even more wet for him.

> You are so tight it feels amazing.

< It looks so good.

> Taste good too I hear

< My pussy wants your tongue.

> I'll lick it up and down
> Inside and out.

< Mmmmmm
< It feels so good.

> I want you to cum on my face.

< I wish you were here RN
< I'm looking at your pic.

< Oh my god
< That was fun
< That pic was perfect

Chapter 4
Conservative Panties

Tues, 1 Aug

3:37 am

6:54 am

Touch me

Ok

Snuggle me

Nic sends me a pic of himself. He's smiling in bed.

> I am in my dreams.

Let me inside of them too.

> That's a great pic.
>
> Oooh I want to snuggle you.

Please do.

> I'm tired.

Me too

And hard AF

> Oooohhhh

Your fault

I send Nic a picture of myself again. I'm lying on my bed and wearing my short grey shorts. My butt is hanging out the bottom just enough to peak his excitement but not enough to reveal too much.

Daddy likes that butt

hee hee

More please

Nic shows me again the effect my words are having on him with a pic of his bulging blue underwear.

Are you wearing panties?

> I am.

> What color

> White

> Conservative or sexy

> Conservative

> That's what I like

> For real? You're just saying that

> I'd rather my mind have some room to think than just show all

> Anything you wear I would melt for.

> 👄👄

Am I gonna have to beg to see your panties
I'll get on my knees.

Ooops. I'm half asleep.

Oh I'll leave you be then.

Hold on.

I send Nic a pic of my lower half with my white conservative undies on and my shirt pulled up just a little.

Mmmmmmmmm
Breakfast of champions.

Time to start the day

> You're gonna make me cum in my shorts.

> Ooohhhh
>
> Have a great day Nic

> You too Love
>
> I want you so bad
>
> Ok sorry chat later
>
> Lol.

Tues, 1 Aug

10:59 am

> You devil

> I want to be your little devil

Please

Would you want to be dominant to me today? Switch roles?

Not sure

This daily pace is a bit too much for me I'm afraid

I can explain more of what I mean when you have time. I don't want to bother you at work.

I just feel I've made you already go too far from where you thought you were comfortable

I want to give you the same chance

I'm not busy today at work so explain if you want.

Yes. I have gone further and faster than I would've predicted with you over text. But I am comfortable with how it's gone so far. I just don't think I can be more dominant than I have been. Sorry about that. And then the other thing is just that the last two nights have been amazing, but I'm sure I can't keep up that pace every night. Momma's tired!

> Now I'm bringing my boys to the dentist. I can talk again soon.

I only was wanting to be fair and see if you wanted some control. No need to apologize.

If you only want to be kinky certain times and not all day. Please just communicate that it won't offend me. I want to do exactly what you want me to do for you.

> You're the best
> So understanding

I'm just trying to have fun and not ruin your career because you can't get work done.

Just let me know ok 😜

> Yes!!! ❤️
> 😋

LATER THAT DAY

> I want a Nic hug

Remember I'm short so it's gonna be around your waist

Ha! I don't care. A hugs a hug 😆

BTW my first love, the guy who took my virginity was shorter than me 👀 ❤️

I'm just closer to the target.

Oh boy 😂

Sorry.

Ha!

I send Nic a pic of myself from above. I'm wearing my green V neck tee shirt and my hair is all curly and wild.

Hey sexy.

Those eyes

Can I request some play time later. Not too long and NOT late.

Play time like the last few nights?

Yes, silly, Virtually. I'm still in hiding mode right

That would be too frequent for me. I'm sorry 😟

> Oh ok I think I get it now. You want more time in between
>
> Speak up please.

>> Yes that's right
>>
>> That's what I thought I was saying earlier today.

> Am I losing your attention?

>> No no
>>
>> You have my full attention.

> I thought you meant throughout the day was too much I'm sorry.

>> I was in heat for days and could barely sleep. I feel better now. Like I got my body back. This means it's best for me to have time in between.

> You can just let me know when you are ready for that again ok. I don't want to be pushy but YOU are going to have to initiate it because that's the introvert in me feeling like I caused an uneasy situation which I know you would say no no. But that's how my brain works.

> You are the sweetest and so F'ing sexy. I'll definitely initiate it. Don't be afraid to do that too if it's been a few days I'll be more likely to be ready.

Good cause I want a little more next time so build up your courage 😉

And don't over think that.

> Mmmmm Ok but it's hard not to over think that.

Tues, 1 Aug

8:20 pm

Like you were real sexy with your last couple pics. I just want to continue that. I'm not asking or wanting to see full nudes is what I mean by don't overthink. I mean it would be nice but I already told you I like my mind to be able to race a little (conservative panties) I hope that makes sense.

> That does make sense. Yes

I really enjoy you and I'm not ever wanting you to think I'm a creep by asking for pics. I will never ask for full nudes I would look at them if sent tho 👀 🤭

>

> I know. I hear ya. Thanks.

THREE HOURS GO BY

> I just went on a walk and then something occurred to me. I think part of my hesitation right now is that I miss our texts that were super flirty and cute but not like sensual. Of course those texts were the ones that got me super hot for you. But they weren't about actual sex. Does that make sense?

Yes Babe we can just have conversations through the day and whenever you feel like you want to be naughty let me know. I am always in the mood sorry 👀 🤣 😉

> Hee hee I gathered that 😂

> Thank you for understanding me.

Ok good. Just communicate it's not going to upset me.

> I love that 🙂 👀
> Same for you too.

> Communication is so important

This just makes me want you more.

But I'll be patient.

The fruit needs to ripen.

Wed, 2 Aug

9:55 am

> Are you at work?

Yes, why what's up?

> Feeling wet for you
>
> Sorry to bother you. We can chat later. I just wanted you to know.

Mmmm

Babe my job is not complex and I am not busy today so you can chat.

> What can I do for you?

> > Really nothing right now. But thank you. I just wanted you to know. I have to get to work. I'm thinking of you though

> Now I'm thinking of your soft skin and cute smiles and those eyes 🥲

> > 🥲

Wed, 2 Aug

3:19 pm

> How is your day?

> > Hi!!!

> WYD

> > Bringing one son to perform at the Wallhaven concert in the park. But I can't stay to watch, instead I have to bring Will to soccer. Then back to Wallhaven to pick up the other one. 😅

#hotmomlife

Wed, 2 Aug

10:00 pm

Ok I want you. What do I have to do?

Have patience.

I have some 😉

laughing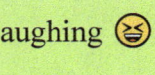

Ooops

I mean

I want you bad tho

But I will wait if I have to.

I'm still playing Nerf guns.

Hell yeah.

> He's winning 🎯

Dig deep Babe
I believe in you.

> ❤️❤️
> Is it lame that I love every one of your texts 🤭

No they are intentional so I get why you do.

> Would you say you are a calculating person?

Very

Stats

Numbers guy 4 sure

Lol 👆

> Then how do I know the real you?

Wait what?

> If you are just texting things that you know I'll like.

> I think I'm tired and reading into things.

Calculating person. I am a numbers guy I run a business I'm a thinker. I calculate.

> I guess by calculating I mean manipulative.

I'm kinda lost if this is meant to be negative

Now I'm thrown for a loop

What am I manipulating?

> I think I just am in awe of how awesome you are. Like I love every text you write.

And you can do that.

> I'm saying how can I love every text from you but I do. You make me laugh every day.

What do you think I'm trying to gain with this?

> I don't know. I just never been won over by text before
>
> It's been fun and wild
>
> I'm in awe

> Is what I'm trying to say.

Just feel it then, I want you to enjoy it

Lust for me.

>
> I do.

Show me.

> Still playing Nerf RN.

Yup. Whenever you can Babe.

> I'm sorry I can't chat tonight. I need to sleep soon ♥ ♥

Thur, 3 Aug

8:24pm

I don't like something you said and feel.

From my weird texts last night?

Yes. I am not trying to manipulate you at all. Of course I want to make love to you. But even if we never meet I thought we were having fun exploring.

You are right. I do believe all that. Last night my skeptical and nervous side came out since this has been very intense for me and I've never done anything like this before.

We do not have to continue

I don't want you to do anything that makes you uncomfortable.

I do want to continue.

> Makes me feel reserved now tho. Not gonna lie. I don't like making anyone uncomfortable.

>> I'm sorry
>>
>> I wonder how we can get past this? This was all so different and exciting that I had to question it a bit.
>>
>> But I do think you are genuine. It's just crazy how good we mesh.

> It's a fantasy.
>
> Can I be your fantasy?

>> Yes
>>
>> But I also want a hug or 2 IRL.

> I would love to meet you, have a glass of wine or two just see the smile in real life. Knowing I connected with you on a level no one has ever.
>
> If we decided to actually make love that would be awesome too. But for me this is just as rewarding.

>> Yes!!!!!
>>
>> I'm glad you're happy with this tho
>>
>> I just think I'm not that good at it for you through texting.

You have no idea what you do for me. Even your smile shots make me happy and you have slowly gotten more edgy which is hot AF. Even your conservative panties

You have made me cum in my shorts. I don't even have to touch myself.

It's all because how you've made me feel. It's all you Babe.

I definitely want that glass of wine with you in a few short weeks.

Let me see you.

I send Nic a selfie with wet hair. I'm wearing a black and white V neck tee shirt and I'm standing against a white wall. I'm smiling with all my teeth.

All over please.

I send Nic a pic of myself from top to bottom. I'm wearing grey leggings and my reading glasses. I have a smirky smile on my face.

Are you in leggings?

Yes Sir

> I want that glass of wine with you NOW.

Aren't leggings a little revealing for you?

>
> My hair was wet in that pic. It's fluffed out now.

Looking good.

> I'm trying to look good for you.

Don't do it for me. Be sexy for you.

> Yes. I agree. It's that sexy confidence that gets me feeling sexy for you. It's like a cycle.
>
> I was thinking about something. I was thinking about the significance of sex in a relationship. It's much more important than I ever thought before. For instance, I knew I was in trouble in my relationship with my ex when I stopped wanting to have sex because the admiration and respect and trust was gone. That was so many years ago and I wish I had listened to those feelings more.

> Sex is like the barometer of a relationship
>
> FYI my phone may die at some point today and my kid took my charger for the day 😢 😡

I want to make you feel special. That is my job as a man.

> Awwww love that.

If you need me to touch you a certain way or hug you or kiss your neck. Just let me know if you want me to tell you how I want to do naughty things to you just let me know.

I want to satisfy you top to bottom with no stone unturned.

> Oh my. Thank you.
>
> Amazing
>
> I want a hug now 😢

Anytime.

> Mmmmmm dreaming of it.

I want a kiss.

YES!!!!!

Starting off very soft.

My kisses are very soft. Almost lady like.

I want one.

Just one?

Yes. Only one. At first

I'm on a zoom call smiling like crazy.

Smart move because all bets are off if we start making out.

Are you at a desk?

> Couch

I bet your ass looks good in those pants.

>

Silly you can share a pic. For proof.

> I thought we weren't going there….

Well don't tease me.

> I can't get a good one.

Use a mirror silly

If you don't want to it's ok.

> I'll try again.

Be sexy silly this isn't a chore.

> I know. I just want it to be good for you.

I have never seen a bad pic from you

Your innocence turns me on for Christ sakes.

>

So pure

Untouched.

> I love that you love that about me.

I want you to cave in a little because I make you feel special but also that you are wanting it too.

> Cave in what way?

You are not usually naughty so when you are it's like you're caving in to your fantasy.

> Ahhh I see
>
> Ok.

> I can see myself doing that at times but not every night. It takes a bit to build up the desire.

Oh I thought I was desirable

So you have a low sex drive?

> You ARE desirable oh my
>
> I'm not sure the level of my sex drive. But in the past few weeks with you, it's been much higher than it has in a long time.

If I could make you wet everyday would you let it happen?

> You already are. I am wet right now thinking about you. Holy sh*t.
>
> It's happening regardless of me wanting to control it
>
> Do you know what that sound is

?

I think I have an idea.
You Alone?
Are you doing my job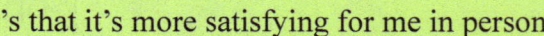

> It's that it's more satisfying for me in person
>
> Not alone

I was humbly telling you I know that sound.

And yes doing your job 😂

Did you squirt?

No

It was still fun tho.

I'm gonna make you squirt one day. I promise.

Have you ever?

I think our texting is breaking my phone.

Water resistant don't worry

I think you're replying but then I can't see your text

I may have left it in the cursor and walked away to mop. Sorry

Have you ever squirted?

I'm not sure. I don't know.

I'll get you there

So you like oral? Giving and or receiving?

I'm also not sure

Chapter 5
Like We've Never Experienced

Thur, 3 Aug

10:10 pm

Hi Babe

WYD cutie

Love your virtual smooches. They make me feel funny in my tummy 🤭

Hanging with Will

He beat me in Nerf again 😭

Lol he's savage.

We're birthday buddies

He's so savage

It's scary

You've had wine.

> I've been having fun imagining our first date
>
> No wine tonight
>
> I almost had some. There you go mind reading again.

I don't want to take time away from Will. So I want you to know if you keep messaging me I'm going to keep responding.

> I hear you. He's next to me on his computer on the couch. So I can chat a bit.
>
> He's gaming.

Tell me about our date

Don't be lame and shy. Tell me the good stuff too

> You love the good stuff I know.

You are the good stuff so yes.

>
>
> You went to charm school I'm sure of it.

Set the table for me, where are we in said date?

> Ok
>
> So. One idea is we meet at a bar…for a few drinks.

> And now I don't mean this to be lame, but that's it for the first date. Then we can of course chat over text when we each get home….
>
> Then the second date we do whatever we want
>
> I would love to flirt at a bar with you one night when we first meet. But that's it. I totally don't mean this to sound lame. It sounds sexy to me.
>
> Your thoughts?

Your wish is my command. As I said before, we don't have to have sex. This is as much of a fantasy for me as it is you.

> Ok. I know. We can see how it goes. No pressure. But I CAN'T WAIT to see you.

I will not lie, I crave to make love to you. I want to fulfill this fantasy like you have no idea.

> I love that. I feel the same.
>
> You are way too fun.

> I am just as impacted as you are in this whole thing. You went from a zero level kink. I went from maybe 3 to 4. We are just on different levels but able to take care of our needs for each other in a way I've never experienced.
>
> I hope that reads well ♥

I love the part you wrote: in a way I've never experienced.

> What if it felt so right to merge the dates. What if you couldn't get in your car and just drive home being so riled up? So hot for what has just happened and you just have to be skin to skin with your fantasy? What if?

Reading. My. Mind.

> Just what if? You don't even have to tell me but you have to wonder 😉

That's exactly the whole fun of that first date fantasy. You totally get it.

> Duh.

>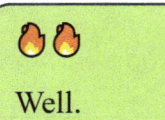
> Well.

I shoulda been a writer like you.

> You could be
>
> I hope I make you smile.

Keep me in mind for a sexy novel.

> I will

I'm grinning right now hard AF.

>
> Yay.

I just wanna see your cute ass in leggings 🤷‍♂️♥

>
> I'm having wine after all.

> Good, now relax.

Yep. Thank youuuuu.

> I've got an idea.

I'm all ears.

> Hear me out. I've had a cocktail or two.

Got it…

Go on

No pressure but my battery is low again. 10% and my son has my charger and he's not home.

Don't worry I read him the riot act for taking it. I was so angry.

> So date one happens and we can't resist.

> But date two happens and starts off like date one but ends early no touch! Date three happens and starts off like date one but can end either like 1 or 2. How will it go?

Omg I have to read that again but slower. Hold on

Oh my!!!!

Ok ummmm.

> Shhhh
>
> Don't tell
>
> It's the hype.

Mmmmmmm

I like that

What bars do you like?

Do you ever go out?

> I don't go out Babe
>
> I message you every nite

I know right

> I am home ALONE
>
> Lol.

Awwwww

Someone touch me 🙅‍♂️ 🤣

You're desperate

I'm here for ya. 🤷‍♂️

Nope I've been chasing this one that I just can't get to yet.

😂

Very shy.

So shy

I don't know how you function so shy

You need to come out of your shell Babe.

I was saying the one I can't get to yet is shy, silly. That's you

I know!!!
❤️

> Out of my shell Miss Conservative Panties

Heeee

Those panties…they need an upgrade

I want to cuddle with you now

I'm sorry to gush over you I can't help it

I feel like a schoolgirl with you.

> Mmmmmmm.

Mmmmmmm.

I want to melt into your arms.

> Like Daddy's little girl?

Yes

So cozy.

> So you will be good for Daddy?

> I'll try but it'll be hard

Oh Babe I'm already hard.

> Mmmmmmm
>
> Heee
>
> You have swept me off my feet

I'll gently lay you down and start kissing you all over like we are 16.

> Ok. Please please do.

I kiss gently just soft to the touch

You are squirming.

> Yes yes yes
>
> You have brightened my life.

That makes me happy.

I need a bigger heart emoji to send you

But they are one size

Don't worry I've got a decent size one for ya

Oooohhhh

Yay.

You never answered if you like to give or receive oral? It's not a trick question.

I do like to receive it. I'm a little iffy on giving it. I'm afraid of diseases.

Does that sound terrible?

I can completely understand.

When my ex and I got together in our 20s we both got AIDS tested

Negative fyi.

> Hippie.

> Right?!?

> Daddy likes hippies lol.

> Good thing!
>
> I'm getting more wine. Hold on Daddy.

> Let me see that butt when you get up to go get that wine.

>
>
> I'm drinking boxed wine because when I bought it I didn't even own a bottle opener
>
> Crazy sh*t

> Nah you're good.

> Thanks.
>
> You are my honey.

I want to taste you.

Mmmmmmm

I'm so excited to have a drinky drink with my honey.

I have a story for you.

Tell me Babe.

Ok

When I lived in D.C.

I took a train to N.Y. to see my mom

With one of my kids

We were waiting

At the platform for the train to leave

I looked out the window of the train

And I saw a man and woman

The man was sitting on the ground

And the woman was sitting on top of him

Straddling him.

> They were embracing
>
> And kissing
>
> And hugging
>
> And she was rocking into him.
>
> It was the hottest thing I've ever seen in public in person. And it was so hot that it was in public and no one cared.

> Do you fantasize about having sex in public?

> Yes. Ever since then.
>
> Isn't that so hot?
>
> I got wet just watching them.

> I want you wet for me
>
> Watch me in my eyes when I'm going down on you.

> Melt.

> You can see the passion I'm enjoying.

> Oh my oh my I can't. It's too much passion. I love it.

> Put your hands on the back of my head for more pressure.

Ok.

> Using ALL of my tongue.

I will

Mmmmmmm.

> Good little girl you are.

Hhhhhhhh

Mmmmmmm.

> Lay with me.

I want to

How did we find each other?

> Well I found you

> You're melting me into a puddle of my former self.
>
> I still think you're not real
>
> No offense.

> I like puddles
>
> On my beard. On my chest and on my cock.

> Mmmmmmmmm

> You are a woman's number one fantasy.

> Maybe I only want to be one's fantasy.

> Sweet or dry wine?

> Dry ❤️❤️

> Like our Sex Life.

> Wait what 😃

> Dry like our Sex Life.

> Ha!!!!!!
> Let's change that
> You are the funniest.

> Let me just put the tip in. 👀 🤣 💨 😈

> Ooooohhhhh tease
> Melt. Total melt.

> You're basically a virgin so I'm gonna be gentle.

> That's so so true. You totally get me.
> You make me so hot.

> Let Daddy pop your Cherry.

Mmmmmmm

What bar should we go to?

> I have two picked out.
>
> Not telling yet.

So hot

Can I even date you before my divorce is final?

I think I can.

> Babe this is a Fantasy. You can do whatever you want.

I want it to be real.

> Not now.

> Let Daddy hold you.

>> Please!!!!!!

> Lay behind you
> Playing with your hair
> Kissing your neck.

>>

> I want to grab the back of your neck and pull you in for a big kiss.

>> Mmmmmmmm.
>> You give me butterflies.

>> I'm so happy about that
>> Because, same
>> Texts like tonight get me so hot for you.

> I want more.

> I want you.

Hug me harder.

> Ok. Hugging harder.

Let me put it in all the way now.

> Ok.

Mmmmmmm.

> I'm ready.

I know what you mean I can feel you.

> Been ready for days.

> I know you can.

Slowly all the way in
And out.

> Yes yes yes please.

Toying with your clit each time I pull out.

> Mmmmmmm
> Ooooooohh

And push it back in.

> Mmmmmm all the way
> I'm pulsating.

Deeper?

> Please
> Please.

> Harder?

> > Yes
> > Yes

> Look at me

> > Ok

> I want to watch you cum while watching your eyes

> > Ooooooooohhhhhhhh
> >
> > I'm gonna have to save these texts for when I need them later
> >
> > This is so hot.

> Later. Fuck me now.

> > I'm on fire.
> > Ok.

Ok.

Fireman 👤

Come to my rescue.

I've got a hose and I know how to use it

I know mouth to mouth.

Am I cut off?

No you're not

Honestly I long for mouth to mouth

I want you so bad.

> You wouldn't last sixty seconds mouth to mouth with me
> Date scenario 2 would happen.

😮
Ok 😃

> I'm very sensual with my kisses.

You may be my dream man
I need a sensual kiss like I need oxygen.

> I'm as close as they come to a lesbian kisser but male.

Mmmmm.

> I think I get what you need and crave.

Yes you do
Clearly.

> Yes Daddy does.

> You melt me.

You don't have to call me Daddy. I thought you were liking it.

> It's fun. Yes.

I don't mean it derogatory.

> I'm dripping with wetness for you
>
> You are saying everything right
>
> As usual
>
> You know what to say.

I want you on top of me like you saw that couple.

> Yes!!!!!!!
>
> This part of me has been dead too long.

I want you to take control

Just for now

And fuck me.

> Ok I will
>
> I will fuck you hard.

Deeper.

> I'm letting you in deeper and deeper and deeper
>
> Amd moving up and down on your cock.

I can feel your pussy gripping my cock.

> Up and down. Gripping tighter and tighter around your cock
>
> Tighter
>
> And tighter
>
> Up and down.

I'm gonna cum if you keep that up.

> Slowly then faster
>
> Then faster and tighter
>
> I want you in me
>
> I want you inside of me.

> It can't get any better of an angle and it's buried in there.

< All the way in.

> You're sooooo wet.

< I'm so so wet
< It's easy.

> Are you touching yourself?

< I'm not but I'm on fire.
< I'm not alone.

> Let me touch you then.

< I want you to cum
< I want to please you.

> Where?

> Inside me.

Is it safe?

> Yes we're safe
>
> I think I need to go find privacy.

Then I will unload in you and fill you up so much you can't walk without making a mess.

> Yes.

Whooops sorry.

> That's ok
>
> I want you to be satisfied.

Find privacy and then find me
I want to see what said privacy looks like.

> Ok. One Second
>
> It's just my tiny bathroom
>
> I can't wait to have you in person
>
> To kiss you.

Are you in privacy?

> Yes.

Let's get down to business

> K

I want you to squirt.

> Ok
>
> I have more success in person. I'm afraid

I agree

But this is different.

> This foreplay is off the charts.

What's the quickest way to cum. Fast? Slow? Soft? Aggressive?

> In person?

Yes in person.

> I'd say slow is the magic formula
>
> And soft.

I'll give ya .36 head start it won't take much longer than that 🦋

>
>
> You are such a man. I love it.
>
> You are rocking my world

That's my JOB.

Am now on another planet. than the one I'm used to

Anus?! LMAO

Ha!!!!

No

Uranus

I gotta put Will to bed

He's on Colarado time still.

I'll be up if you want to see me.

You are the answer to my dreams

Ok

Night night 😊

Halloween is coming up. If you had to dress me up, what costume would you choose? 🔥

Fri, 4 Aug

8:42 am

Schoolgirl.

You got it.

I agree.

I want you so bad.

Same.

Do you have a skirt? Cute top and long socks or stockings?

No but I will.

No panties? 😉 🤣

That's right.

> Can I just bend you over a desk or chair and have my way, gently and soft of course.

>> Yes. I also need you on top of me.

> Absolutely I'll toss you in the bed and go down and tongue your sweet spot just for a minute before I penetrate you.

>> Now

> Yes

>> I love it so much

> My cock is throbbing for you and it's only 9:15 AM

>> Mmmmmmm.

> I just want to please you and make you feel like ecstasy.

> Yes
>
> I'm touching myself.

Please do in my absence.

> Ok

Take care of it for Daddy.

> Ok

How many fingers?

> One is best.

That's right baby girl
Nice and tight right.

> Very
>
> No babies went through there.

> Mmmmmm. And no good dick either.

> That's right.

> Now Daddy's here to solve that problem
>
> Little deeper with that finger now
>
> Get the juices flowing.

> Can't type

> I hope you are orgasming and not interrupted.

> Yesssss

> Finish strong for Daddy
>
> Faster
>
> Harder
>
> I wanna hear it
>
> Faster

> I want u here inside me.

Put that finger all the way in and use a circle pattern like I'm circling my hips.

Slowly

Side to side

> K

Open your sweet spot so my cock can squeeze in there.

> I need it.

Are you wet?

> Soooooo wet

How are you touching yourself now?

> I'm straddling you. Rubbing up and down.

You like riding Daddy.

> You're my principal. I was late for school.

Bad girl

> I'm in trouble

You better ride that cock harder then to make up for your tardiness.

> Yes
>
> Every time I'm late I have to go in to your office.

Harder and faster. You have control of the flow but you are in debt to me and being punished.

> Yes
>
> I'll try to never be late again.

> That did it 😋
>
> Mmmmmm
>
> Thank you my love
>
> I'm sorry I didn't let you hear it
>
> Have a great day.

It's ok about not hearing.

You too

My shorts are wet now.

> Ooooohhhhh
>
> Time to get in that shower for us

Wash up real good for Daddy

Let me see you in your towel so relaxed and complete.

I send Nic a selfie after I get out of the shower. My hair is wet and pulled back. I have a big smile on my face with my lips closed. So satisfied.

Clean as a whistle

Next time you're late it's gonna be a little different young lady.

It's not gonna be just a slap on the wrist.

Ooh the plumber is here 😂

Gotta let him in.

That's fucked up. Lol. Cock block

Ok I'll stop. Chat later.

Hee hee. Ok. Chat later.

ONE HOUR GOES BY

I feel like going to your work right now and giving you a nice long sweet kiss. (Don't worry I won't) 💋

I know the perfect hiding spot.

Ooooohhhh even more tempted.

You wouldn't be able to keep quiet.

You know me inside and out now.

I am trying.

You're succeeding.

I want to taste you.

> Mmmmmmmm.

Did you fuck the plumber or saving it for me?

> Def saving it ALL for you.
> You make me feel sexy
> I want you.

You can have me.

>
> You earned it.
> You worked so hard for me.
> You've been so understanding.

Daddy likes to earn his treasures.

>

I thought we weren't supposed to chat

I know 😱 some days I can't help myself with you

Plus today I'm writing about tax law. Needless to say it's not keeping my attention

Get some work done and Daddy can play in awhile.

K

Fri, 4 Aug

2:05 pm

Wanna play in 10 minutes? I'll have a few minutes before I get my kiddos.

I'm at an appointment with my son now.

It's ok there will be plenty of time. I was just trying to fulfill your midday appetite.

Thank youuuuuu ♥

Maybe I'll just have to fend for myself this time

☹

Chapter 6
Did You Drop From Heaven?

Fri, 4 Aug

6:43 pm

I'm hot for you

I was just thinking the same thing

We are on the same wavelength

I'm telling you

You Alone?

No

Ok

> No Will is leaving soon for Colorado. That will change my whole life. I can't believe it.

Ok I know I can't even imagine. I know I don't talk about it but I feel for you in this situation. It breaks my heart. I tried to stay in New Mexico longer than my kids after the divorce before I moved back to Ohio and it destroyed me.

> So they moved here with your ex and then you followed after at some point?

So she asked to move back for the kids to be with family. I had a lease obligation until Nov. they moved back in July. I also came back for a wedding in July and when I went back to New Mexico after the wedding, I just couldn't wait until Nov to move back and didn't want to be without them. So I came back in August.

> Wow
>
> So you're both from here but you were both in New Mexico? If I'm ever asking too much just say so and I'll stop.

Nope I'm an open book. We are from here. I was promoted and transferred to New Mexico in 2013 for 7 years.

> Oh ok.

> Maybe our first date can be next weekend?

When does Will go to Colorado?

What about the twins?

> Will goes Sunday but maybe Tuesday. Most likely Sunday.
>
> Twins stay here with me. I'm hoping we can hang at your place if we ever want to be in private

This sunday? He goes?

> Yep. It got very moved up. I'm freaking out.

Oh I'm sorry

> ♥
>
> Schools starts earlier there and I want him to be ready

> And yes I can always host for privacy. I don't live in a mansion but a bachelor apartment

> In case your fantasy had marble countertops and 1000 thread count sheets
>
> Just don't want to let you down

All it needs is you

> All it needs is US and freedom to do whatever we want.

YES

> You make me so hard

Awwww 👄
I love how we mesh

> I'll count the ways…
>
> Same birthday. Divorced of course. Twins. You read my mind. You totally get me…
>
> You're hotter than hell

> You text me things that I was already thinking
>
> We both just want ♥ love ♥ without drama

That's the best kind

So there's no negative vibe in the background. It's all positive and just a make love vibe, relax and just let whatever happens, happen. Like Vegas but cheaper

> Yes yes yes
>
> Love it
>
> You have no idea how you're brightening some shitty days for me lately.

That's my job. I am your fantasy

> Did you drop from heaven?

I suspended down like Tom Cruise in Mission Impossible

> I think you did

I want you to open up just a little more again

> I can

I know you can but do you want to?
I'm not being weird

> I do want to

I'm pushing your boundaries

Yes you are

So you have some hard NO's and I'll always follow them.

Tell me a soft no or two that you would like to try but you think may be uncomfortable to do because of insecurities or have never tried.

I don't know at the moment. Can we revisit this? We're about to start an epic Nerf battle.

Yes. I'm going to play volleyball now. I want you to cross the line with me. Try new things that you want to explore.

I LOVE VOLLEYBALL

Jealous

I bet you look good in a volleyball outfit

Can we play? Later. I really need some of you.

> Yes

Please I really need you

> Yes Yes. For sure

Fri, 4 Aug

9:30 pm

Aren't you 48?

> No.

How old?

I'm watching a show and it made me think of why I first matched with you!

> I'm scared to tell you

No please I think it will be very good for you

> 50

So I am very much into older women.

I think that's why I originally matched with you. I mean yes you are beautiful but I don't get along with immature girls. I mean Daddy wants his baby girl but that's different

>
> Don't take this the wrong way but I feel like you're older than me. You know what I mean

It's because I've been teaching you exactly what you need to know and want

> Yes

I'm your leader

> Yes

You obey me

> You slay me

I get what I want

> Mmmmmm Breathless.

But I want you to enjoy in the fun too

> I am ♥
> I'm about to make sundaes with Will.

Ok chat soon.

> Yes

I crave you.

> And I you
> I can't wait for our bar date

> You can show Daddy how much later via pics 😉
>
> You're not gonna be able to contain yourself in public

>> I know 😆

> Go make sundaes. I'm hard AF RN.

>> Mmmmmmm

> I'll show you a little later how hard I am

>> Mmmmmmm

> Not the whole thing creeper

>> Oh ok 😆

> I'm shy ya know
>
> Ok go. Chat soon

I don't think you're shy though

> I can talk a bunch of shit. I'm way more conservative than I present myself here to you.

That's hard to believe

I'm sorry

I guess you're shy in person?

> I'm horrible at the first move and I can't read the room right
>
> I don't spank women unless they ask me to I see it as violence

Why do some people like spanking

Pain isn't pleasure to me

> I think there are two sides. Man maybe shows heightened aggression letting her know he's already all the way in deep and asking her for more 🤷‍♂️

I think I want things between us to be more traditional in the bedroom than what you want. Do you think?

> Nope. I'm a basic guy. I love hot steamy sex. I don't want to tie you, gag you, piss on you or wear a mask.

PHEW!! Lol

> I want to make you cum in the most simple ways.

I like that answer.

> I want to whisper to your skin and get you goosebumps

Oh my god yes

I can't wait for you

> Is the bar date a bad idea?!?
>
> Like, who are we kidding?
>
> I just want to see you in normal circumstances I guess. Then see what happens

We can decide the specifics of the date the day before. That way no one has an upper hand on the outcome

> That's good. But what do you mean by the last sentence?

I mean like the sexy scenarios on the outcome of like date one and 2. Like we just don't know so it's a level playing field

> Ok. Got it
>
> What show were you watching earlier?

It was a reference to Cougar Town. And I thought that's how my original kink for you was– you are older.

> Ok.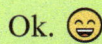

> You were leaning on a balcony or like a fence. All innocent and shit. I knew you were kinky AF

In a picture?

> Yes your profile pic

With water in the background

> Show me

Ok hold on

I send Nic a picture from my Facebook profile. I'm leaning against a low rock wall that is bordering a river in the background with a big blue sky above.

> Yeah that one

I'm not kinky though

I don't think

> Ummm do you need to review the transcripts
>
> Or you mean looking?

Oh oops. Maybe I am.

I don't know what that word truly means

How can we text so many hours? It's so fun. I'm so excited to just hang with you.

> You are pinup girl material. Hot silent sexy not trying to draw attention but you have ALL of mine

Your words light me on fire

> Let me stoke your coals 😊

> That was good right lol

You are a wordsmith

I have to go pick up Ethan from work. Be back soon to chat.

> I want to see you. I want to play a little
>
> Chat soon

Yes I want to too

> Pull yourself together 🤭

Hee hee

> Chat soon

K

I'm driving in the car right now and just wondering what is some music you like that I can put on Spotify?

I respect that question and we won't align in real life in music. Let's be honest. So I will just speak in our fantasy terms.

We talked a little about this before. Seriously, what music do you like?

I like so much different music that it's bound to match up at least a little

I love blues, jazz and classical. I love on Sundays they play pipes and organs and highlight what church or venue it's at

How fucking nerdy to even care where the organ is in the world but I find it interesting

I love your nerdy side

Sometimes I like lyrics to songs sometimes the vibe from the beat

OK. Chat soon. Ethan and his friends are getting in the car.

shhhhhh

> Ha
>
> Yes. Shhhhh

I wish I was between your legs while driving

Chat soon

LATER THAT NIGHT

> I wish you were too
>
> I've had that fantasy about you more than once–while I'm driving
>
> It's unreal how you read me and know me

You keep avoiding the soft No's

> I don't mean to
>
> I don't know how to answer

You Alone?

> No
>
> I'm on the couch. I can text
>
> My ex will be bringing my son home soon

> My bedroom door in my apartment doesn't lock
>
> So everyone has to be tucked away before I do naughty stuff in there
>
> Do you live in Highland Square like your license says?

Yes Highland Square. Why would you think I'm lying?

> I don't. Licenses don't lie. They just aren't always current

I'm current and no diseases so you can suck my cock with no hesitation

> Mmmmm
>
> Oh my

So I think this is a soft no for you

Hesitation

Not experienced

> Yes

> So why not just type it when I ask. Why do I have to pull it out of you?
>
> Just a flirting question

Type what?

> Type what is a soft NO when I ask?

Because I don't know what to even say to that question

> Maybe let me reword it
>
> Is there a sexual position, fantasy, thought that you would like to come true but not sure how to go about it?

I think no.

> So you have experienced all of your naughty thoughts and desires?

Hold on

Yes dear

> Still hold on
> Nerf moment

Sniper
Savage

> Still Nerfing

It's ok. I'll be up waiting for you to pounce

>

Are you up for the task?

> Yes

Ok see you soon
Don't be late

> I hope it's not too late

Try to give me a heads up so I can prepare

> Ok

Don't be late was the reference of punishment – not being serious

> Ooooohhh hee hee
>
> Will wants to play with me late every night and ignores me all day

Lol just like Daddy

>
> But now I just want to crawl in bed with you

Please do

> I want to

> I'm sorry I'm so hard

> > I think we're only playing a bit more
> > It's too late for him

> Ok Let me know when you're ready
> I'm gonna rock your world

> > I'll end it with him very soon
> >

> Apologizing now the later it gets the more intense my thoughts become

> > I'll be ready in a few

30 MINUTES GO BY

> > Here for you when you need me
> > Did I lose you to sleep?

> I'm here now

> Oh good
>
> I was getting worried

Can Daddy have you now?

> Yes

All of you?

> Yes

> Ru still hard for me?
>
> Where's my Daddy?

Nic sends me a picture of his underwear.

> There he is

I want a pic please

> Of what?

I want to see more skin. Doesn't have to be graphic just be sexy

I send Nic a selfie while I'm laying in bed wearing a black V neck tee shirt.

> Ok

Stop trying to get the perfect shot just give me you

> Oh my goodness
>
> I want to rub up and down against you
>
> My pussy and your cock rubbing together
>
> Do you want me?
>
> Did you not like the one I sent?

I didn't get any pic

> I'll send it again

Ma'am are you playing with me?

I send it again.

> I hope I didn't send it to someone else
>
> Did you get it?
>
> I sent 2

> Ok got em both
>
> Nice cleavage
>
> Was that on purpose?

Yes

> Don't be shy let me see some more

K.

I pulled my shirt down

Nic sends me a selfie from his bed. It's dark in the room and he has a sexy look on his face.

> omg sexy

I muster the courage (and heat) to send Nic a pic of my boobs.

Nic sends me a selfie of his face and bare chest. His chest is just the right ratio of hair to skin.

> I want to play with those
>
> You are so sexy

> Show me more. Stop being so shy. It's just me
>
> I want to put my cock in between them

> You can

Will it fit?

I'll make room

Will you lick the tip while I titty fuck you

Yes

I will

I want to see your panties

K

I send Nic a pic of my white conservative panties.

> I want to be right there

>> Yes

> You have so many clothes on
> Get naked with me

>> I can't
>> I'm sorry

> Yup no worries

>> Can we get back to the hot words
>> Instead of pics

My cock is throbbing. I just need to know where you want it

> Put it deep inside
>
> It'll slide right in

Is Momma all wet for me?

Is she really ready now?

> So so ready. Been ready for Daddy all day
>
> Been ready and wet all day

Let me penetrate that pussy like you've been begging for it all day

I want you to relax

> Please

> And just get fucked
>
> Take it

>> Yes
>>
>> Come into me
>>
>> I'm helpless
>>
>> My pussy is yours

> In and out

>> Yes

> I want to pull it out slowly

>> Kiss me

> And slap your clit with my dick toying with you
>
> Oh I'm always kissing you I can't keep my lips off of you

> Mmmmmm
>
> My pussy needs you

I'm gonna scoot you to the edge of the king size bed to get a better angle

Deeper

> Yes
>
> Deep and
>
> Slow

I want to pull it out so slow I feel your pussy trying to pull it back in even every last try on the tip of my cock

> Yes

And just push it back in

> Yyyyessss

Your eyes have rolled into your head

> Fuck me hard

I know how vulnerable you are

> My legs are wide open

Yes spread em and just take the pounding

> Yes

I want you to squirt all over me

The sound of hitting it right

Mmmmmmm

> My pussy is grabbing you

Can you handle this cock

> No

Am I too much for baby girl?

> Yes
> I just came hard

Mmmmmm
I wish I could taste it

> Mmmmm
> So satisfied

Are your fingers sticky?

> They were
>

Did you taste them?

> No

Hey now some girls like that

> I'm sure

Next time I want to taste that tho

> 😊I know

And I promise to get in deeper too

> Ok

And harder

> Yes

> How do you feel about two dicks inside of you?

Are you referring to a 3 some?

> Nope
> Just answer the question

No

> Ok

How would that work?

> It was question if you would enjoy that

I don't get it
A dildo?

> I would never have a threesome with another guy. If you felt a craving yes I guess a dildo. Or toy of some sort. I've never done that. It was just a question on what you desire

Ok

You are very sexual

More than me

> I didn't know if it's something you thought about

Nope

> Again I'm trying to get those soft NO's So I bring up the hard ones. Lol

Interesting tactic

> Keeping your mind intrigued and your pussy wet
>
> Send me a pic please

> I can't do any more pics
>
> I'm sorry

No worries. I wish you felt more comfortable. I mean no harm

> It's that plus I'm so tired and the flash or light is too bright

Sorry to keep you up too late and bore you

Sweet dreams

> Omg not bored
>
> But tired
>
> Sweet dreams

I'm so hard for you RN

Sat, 5 Aug

9:12 am

I'm sorry I fell asleep so fast

It's ok

Were you too busy pleasing me that you couldn't please yourself?

Kinda
I'm used to it tho

I was hoping you were getting off like I was

I'm always going to aim to please you first

That is so hot

You're turning me on again

That's why I'm here

> I know. I love it. You're so damn hot. I have to start my day now and get my son to work. It's my last day with Will and I'm worried I'm not going to make it through.

You will be fine. Make memories. Chat later

I'm so confused so he leaves tomorrow?

I thought next Sunday??

> No tomorrow. That's why I asked for a date with you for next weekend.

Go make memories

Sun, 6 Aug

12:00 am

WYD

> You think of me right when I'm thinking of you

I've been wanting you all day but respectfully noting what you are going through

> Thank you. It's been a very emotional day

I can imagine

I'm sorry

> Thanks ❤️❤️
>
> He stays up late so I'm staying up late with him. I don't want to say goodbye to him.

I'll be up Babe I'm here for you

> Thanks 😊

Touch me.

> I can't tonight. I'm sorry.

Sun, 6 Aug

5:58 am

> No worries.

Sun, 6 Aug

7:34 am

> Morning Babe. Sending hugs to you

Sun, 6 Aug

11:00 am

> Morning ❤️❤️ thank you. I got the hugs

> I can't even imagine what your heart is going through

> It's the absolute worst and I'm regretting this decision so badly

> I'm so sorry. But you said it's what Will wants right?

> Yes. But he's sad to leave his brothers

Yes that is normal if he wasn't sad that may be a problem

What time does he leave? Plane? Car?

> Car. Between 1 and 2 pm
>

Hugs Babe

I truly feel your pain

He will be ok.

>

Sun, 6 Aug

5:22 pm

You ok?

> It's really bad. I'm a mess. Ty for checking. It's gonna be a rough week.
>
> My whole life has just changed

> And I'm so mad at my ex for creating this situation.

I'm here if you need to vent.

> Thank you so much

Is Will going to be happy there?

> We believe he's going to be very happy there. He was there for six weeks this summer and absolutely loved it. His biggest problem is missing his brothers. He really didn't want to leave them today.
>
> I think I'm going to sneak into the Barbie movie right now. Just going to follow all the girls in pink. Fuck it.

If he will be happy then Momma should be happy. Keep those boys talking via text, zoom whatever so they don't lose the bond

> Yes exactly. Good advice. The bond is so important.

> Take a breath. Grab a glass of wine

Mon, 7 Aug

1:21 am

> You awake?

Mon, 7 Aug

8:55 am

> Good morning

10:18 am

< Morning

> It's a new day Babe

< Yes. Today's starting a little better than yesterday but I still feel the heaviness in my heart

Absolutely and if you didn't it wouldn't be normal

Mon, 7 Aug

1:46 pm

Do you need a hug?

Yes

I'm off work 😉

Nic sends me a selfie. He's wearing his orange work tee shirt and he's sitting in a truck.

> Awwwww
>
> I'm still working and I'm behind which really sucks

> Take a breath. You will catch back up. I'll leave you be and reach out when you can 😋

> Thanks. I will 😋

Mon, 7 Aug

9:36 pm

> I can't stop thinking about you. I know you are struggling in one headspace and not even thinking about ours but maybe that's what would help you get your mind off of it I just want to be there for you

> I'd like to chat later but I'm not in the right frame of mind to be sexy yet. I know what you mean that it might help. And I know that it will. But today's not the day I'm afraid.
>
> I'm sorry 🥺

No need to be sorry I'm just trying to be here for you

Thank you. You are very definitely being here for me 💕 I'll be back to my old self sooner than later.

Old self
Baby girl I know you will come back stronger than ever

Tues, 8 Aug

9:48 am

Thank ❤ you ❤

9:42 pm

Wed, 9 Aug

2:53 pm

Babe I haven't forgotten about you 💕 I'm sorry to be MIA.

I'm respecting your space. I've been crazy busy at work. Daddy misses his baby girl tho not gonna lie 😌

I'm ready with open arms whenever you are comfortable

Wed, 9 Aug

10:45 pm

You up?

Thur, 10 Aug

10:13 am

Hey. It's been rough this week. I'm neck deep into job searching 😔

Oh no. I don't know what writers do to find jobs but I'm sure you will find something you seem great at your job 🤷‍♂️

Thur, 10 Aug

12:29 pm

Thanks. It's brutal. I need a higher paying gig or a full time job in the next few weeks. 😔

There are lot of jobs out there.

Yes. I'm hoping to get one in a marketing agency though. Get my foot in the door. We could start writing our books and publish 😋 😊

Nic sends me a selfie from work. There are walls of boxes stacked up behind him and he's wearing his orange work tee shirt with an apron over it.

Thur, 10 Aug

4:30 pm

Hi cutie

How's baby girl?

I'm ok. Sorry to be so distant.

No it's ok. I just don't want to lose my spot in line

> I love how you put things. I promise you won't.

Thur, 10 Aug

9:19 pm

Talk to me. Vent to me. I'm here to listen

Breathe

Fri, 11 Aug

10:00 am

I have an open schedule this weekend no work and no kids. Am I still penciling you in??

> Not this weekend. I'm sorry. I'm overwhelmed with my court date next week and job hunting. I'm sorry that I'm backing out of our original plan.

It's ok. Just know that I have made time for you.

> I really appreciate that. I've met you in the middle of a crazy time in my life.

Life never becomes not crazy. It's how we deal with it and also allow time for positive things and even new things. We had a vibe going and I just don't know if you want it to be there or not so I'll leave you be.

Fri, 11 Aug

2:53 pm

> You are right. After Will left I got into a different head space. I don't want to say goodbye though.

If you don't think I have shit I'm going through too you are crazy. But I crave to please and that's what I am going to do. If you stay stagnant this train doesn't stop. It's hard to keep my attention for long. You have done a good job but I think you have moved off of the feeling and don't desire our talks anymore and that's ok. I'm not pushing an agenda.

2:53 pm

> I'm having a really hard time. Please don't take this personally. I'm a mess. I was in a really happy place when I met you. And I was really open for my new life but I've backslided.

I want to help. I want to be there for you. We have shared some deep stuff. The least I can do is to be there for you. It's not all about sex. I told you I need a connection if it's going to lead to sex and I want communication with you if it's not going to lead to sex. It's not all about sex but yes that was our end goal but I crave something deeper for that to happen. I want to be there for you as a friend even if we never meet face to face. You have helped me in ways I haven't shared. You make me feel good. I just want to repay the favor. Sorry if that's too deep but I'm just being honest and open. I thought that's where we were.

That is where we were. Yes, I'm just so sad about my life right now. I was feeling so social a few weeks ago. Now I feel hurt and damaged. Like I don't have it in me to flirt like we used to. I just want to cry. And that's not what you want. You need a happy flirty girl. Thank you for saying you want to help me. I just don't know what help I need.

Sat, 12 Aug

8:38 am

Damnit snap out of it. I'll be here for you even in the darkest days. But you need to focus on you again. Your happiness. I have no problem focusing on you to help you through these times. Everyone needs someone just to talk to, pretty sure I have already filled those shoes. I want you in the worst way. I want to fulfill your needs and wants. I am here.

Sun, 13 Aug

9:33 am

Nic sends a selfie of his face and his bare chest. He's lying in bed.

Sun, 13 Aug

9:04 pm

I hope you are well. Be strong. Tomorrow starts a new week.

11:55 pm

Thank you!

I miss you

Nic sends me a screenshot from Spotify of the song: Need You Tonight by INXS.

I love INXS!!

How did I know?

Chapter 7
Another Crazy Cat Lady

Mon, 14 Aug

7:23 pm

I got a kitten

I send Nic a pic of Harris, my new kitten. He's cuddling with his little lamb stuffed animal.

I send Nic another pic of my kitten. He's standing in front of his scratching post. He's got long whiskers and pink ears and a pink nose.

> Christ now I have more competition

> I want your attention

Mon, 14 Aug

10:41 pm

I'm sorry. I'm still working and trying not to get distracted by Harris. I need to be / feel truly on my own and not like I have a boyfriend. I'm really sorry.

> Yuck a boyfriend I just wanted to fuck you
>
> Hello pay attention
>
> Lol silly little girl
>
> I hope you find what you need
>
> If you ever crave me like you did at one time you know where to find me. I won't bother you anymore. But just know I wanted to satisfy you like you have never had before.

Tues, 15 Aug

1:04 am

I'm only saying boyfriend because the frequency was getting too much for me. Thank you for understanding. I'll stay in touch.

I'm seeking a FWB from you. Not commitment. I appreciate you and all you are going through but I can't give you girlfriend status. I hope we can stay in touch.

Tues, 15 Aug

9:33 pm

I hear ya. I'll be in touch.

I hope so from everything we have been through together

Wed, 16 Aug

10:43 pm

How's the kitten?

> Thur, 17 Aug

3:06 pm

> He's good. There's been a bit of peeing on the bed which is a bummer. But other than that he's really good.

I send Nic still another pic of my kitten. He's laying on the bed with a bunch of white blankets surrounding him.

> I miss you.

> I miss you too.

> How's the job hunting going?

> It's a huge pain in the butt and very discouraging.

> I'm sorry. If there's anything I can do let me know.
>
> Let me see you!

I send Nic a selfie. I'm sitting up in bed with my head against the wall and some pillows. I'm wearing a black shirt and showing a half smile.

That's what I'm looking for

I send Nic a pic in the same position as the pic a minute ago but this time I have Harris on my chest who is looking right into the camera with his tongue sticking out.

Do you see his face?

Feisty like Momma

You know what I'm talking about
🤣🤷‍♂️😈❤️👀

Thur, 17 Aug

8:58 pm

No I do 😆

Whoa we don't say those words Babe. Remember?

I do 😆🤣

Babe you can't keep saying it

You don't even want a boyfriend 👀👀👀

🤷‍♂️🔥🔥😈😈

True 💯

> Just kiss me already
>
> Can I tell you a fantasy I had about you

Yes

> Wait I have a question first
>
> Have we ever talked on the phone before?

No

> Ok ready for the fantasy?

Yes

> So there is a wine bar in Fairlawn that's one of the two places I have an idea to take you to, following?

Yes

> I know we have lost touch in our kinky ways and talks. So I'm wondering how can I get back to that? So I wanted you to go to that bar. I order your wine for you because I made this arrangement. The bartender delivers it and she knows how bad I want to be there with you. But it's not time yet
>
> At that same time we are sexy chatting as if I am in the same room

Such a cool and sexy fantasy mister

> I have more fantasies about you but those are mine sorry 😋

Hee hee

> It's amazing how in tune I am to a fantasy that touches your soul

Yes it's unreal

> I drop the kids off at 8:00 Sunday if you wanna meet, we can. If not forget I mentioned this but I'm gonna try again soon.

> This weekend I've got kids stuff filling the days. But please keep trying. I'm warming back up slowly.

Or better yet meet me virtually at the bar on Sunday. I crave your attention again. I'm so happy 🤣🤷‍♂️

> I can't do that this weekend. But another time soon.

Ok Babe I wasn't demanding this weekend I was just kinda emphasizing my mood for you

> Ok.
>
> I get ya

Butterflies 🦋 is what you give me

THREE HOURS GO BY

> You awake?

Awwww

I am

I'm texting my friend Laura about the messed up state of the world

> Come get lost with me. Not the world.
>
> Then you can tell Laura about that if you want to
>
> 😂

Ha!!!!

> I bet we could get her mind going just with our interactions 👀 😾 🔥 😂 🤪 🤷‍♂️

Ha! I'm sure

> Can I get a selfie?

I send Nic a selfie. I'm laying in bed and Harris is laying on my chest with his body surrounding my neck. I'm giving a small smile.

Now I'm jealous 😊

I'm sorry

I'd love to be on your shoulder
Relaxed AF

Yes....

Knowing I'm there for you

> Have you been in communication with the youngest?

> You TRULY TRULY can read my mind.

> What?

> I'm so sorry ♥

> Does Will not have his own phone?

> I was going to get him one that just calls and texts, but I have not found one in existence
>
> We do email though and of course talk on the phone

> Just keep the communication going for him. I'm sure he misses momma too

> He didn't act like it. But that's ok. I want him to be happy.

He is becoming a Man.

Sometimes we struggle showing our emotions because we are taught not to

> True yes.
>
> Who teaches that? Movies?

Society

> I didn't teach that to my boys but they learned it anyway
> Yeah

I want to kiss you

> Same

But I want mine to radiate through your body

> It will

You better stop

This is kinda hot, eh?

> Yeah. It's just the speed I can handle for now
>
> I love our connection
>
> Thanks for being patient with me lately

Babe you have been there for me. How could I not repay the favor?

Kiss me

I have one small request. If you ever want to text me to see if I am available, just make it like hey how are you or something low-key like that. I think you already do that. But I just wanted to mention it because the boys had my phone for a few hours talking to Will. And I was nervous that you'd maybe text and then I'd have to explain. I think you already do what I'm asking anyway.

I hear you. I'll always check in before we get into chatting

Perfect. Thank you.

Fri, 18 Aug

9:49 pm

I send Nic a short video of my bare feet perched next to a raging fire pit on the patio of a restaurant. You can hear the crackling of the fire and live jazz music playing in the background.

Wow where is that?

We're at Noble Beast Brewing Company in Cleveland.

Who's we and why ain't it WE?

Kidding. Glad you are out

It's me and my sonny boy. He's performing on the patio.

How awesome

I send Nic a pic of my son's jazz group playing outside at night surrounded by the twinkling lights of the restaurant's patio.

Like a personal concert

Wish I was holding your hand

Me too

Are you relaxed?

No. I have a headache and I'm about to drive home from Cleveland. But thanks for asking.

Are you relaxed? Maybe once you get home I can help you relax be safe driving 🤷‍♂️

Sat, 19 Aug

9:21 am

Morning

Sun, 20 Aug

10:52

Hi there !

> Hi

WYD. I was following orders on the initial question security measures 👀 ❤️

> Thank you. That was perfect.

You ok?

> I'm just ok. Really missing Will. He just talked to the twins. I told him I missed him and had to ask him if he missed me. I'm afraid he doesn't.

He is a young man. He is wired not to say that. He doesn't want to show you weakness. This is a serious conversation that I hate to have via text. It is very important that you hear me on this.

> I do get it.

Mon, 21 Aug

4:43 pm

😗

😗 But naughty first text mister 😁

Oh snap. Sorry

That's not naughty

But I get it. Sorry

No harm done. 😁 Just a reminder.

I send Nic a selfie as I'm sitting on my apartment balcony wearing my black bathing suit. I allow some cleavage to show in the picture, my hair is up and I have on a cute little smile.

Going to the pool for the first time all summer

Are you kidding me with the cleavage Babe? Put those puppies away 👀 ❤️ 😉

😂😂

One day I'll be lucky enough to see them

Yes

Do I have to beg?

Please don't make me beg

I don't want you to beg

It'll happen

Mmmmm. Don't make promises you can't keep

I hear ya

But I'm not

I'm just razzing you

I send Nic a pic of my bare legs crossed and relaxing on a pool lounge chair. You can see some of the blue water of the pool in the background.

> Now you are just plain ole teasing me
> Will those wrap around my head

Maybe

> Can you put those toes by your ears

Ha!
I don't think so

> You better start stretching

> You Alone?

> I am. I'm reading at the pool.

Want me to come swim with you?

I'm totally not serious

Just trying to connect again with you

> I did think of that actually

What part?

> You coming here to my pool

Oh YOUR pool eh

I would say meet me in the deep end but it's over my head

> Lies

Ouch.

> Tell me more.
>
> I want to kiss your inner thighs. No sex. Just touch

Omg yes

Now you're teasing….

> No I'm telling you what I want 😈 😋

Mmmmmm

I like the sound of it

> Those legs look so smooth and untouched

Yes

> Do you have a conservative bathing suit on?

Yes Always

> Can I see?

> It has a little skirt

> You know I like that, right?

> Yes

I send Nic a selfie wearing my black bathing suit with the little skirt. You can see my thighs and a little bit of my chest.

> Mmmmmm
>
> I didn't realize how big your boobs are

>

> I bet those are perky and untouched too

> Yes

> You are making me hard BTW. Good thing I have an apron on

Are you at home?

> At work. Silly I don't wear aprons around the apartment

Oh I'm sorry to bother you at work

> Babe. It's slow here. You are not bothering at all. If I couldn't chat I would let you know.

> Where do you live? Fairlawn?

Yes

> Oh where do the kids go to school? Fairlawn High?

Yes

> I went there

> Oh funny

Are they home?

> When I was 16 I was never home. They are home way more than I ever was. I take it as a compliment 😃

Yeah well they are cock blocking me RN so…..

>
> I switched lawyers today so I'm all f'd up

What do you mean switched? What do you mean fucked up?

> I mean I changed to a different lawyer. I'm just f'd up bc it was a big decision. I'm really fine. It was just a big day.

I thought maybe you had some wine and you were fucked up

I was definitely gonna be a pool boy then on my way home 🤣

> Awwww
>
> Harris gets fixed tomorrow so I have to be up early to bring him in. So probably no wine for me tonight sadly

I won't keep you out too late. I'll have you tucked in at a decent time

We have never spoke on the phone have we?

> No

How do you feel about that?

> I'm ok with it for now
>
> I want to see you first
>
> Plus I can hardly talk on the phone anyway. Someone's always here.

What do you mean? See me first before talking on the phone?

> Yea. When I see you that's the first time hearing you. How do you feel about it?

I think that's HOT 👀

What if I have a squeaky voice? 😄

> I doubt it…wait…do you? 😄

No. I have what I've been told a healing voice

What if I show up with the right cologne on and the smell you can't get it out of your head like ya just need to inhale it ya know take a breath? 😄

> I would LOVE that.

I know

> I know you. I've been paying attention
>
> I don't know you but I know some things you crave

> Yes you do
>
> It's incredible
>
> I'm having that glass of wine now

> Be a good little girl. Just breathe

> Yes

> Come closer and snuggle
>
> I missed you

> 😊

> I still want underwear and skinny shirts on both of us but as much skin to skin as possible

> That will be difficult to endure but very very fun

> If you want to break the rules you can. I'm trying to be a gentleman still. It's only 8:21 🤭

> Good point.
>
> I love talking with you.

> I'm glad to be an impact in your life.

> You truly are
>
> You helped talk me through the whole Will thing quite a bit
>
> So much so that for about a week or so if I saw a text from you I would start crying about Will.
>
> Because I felt your comforting thoughts, even just seeing a text from you.

> I just feel the need to be there for people. Not a lot of people but the ones that are super intentional.

> I'm here for you not only for fun and kinky stuff but as a mind, heart, body and soul.

I still want to kiss your thighs tho

You can

Inside and out

Yes please

Maybe if I talk too much you can just grab the back of my head and place it between your thighs to get me to shut up

Maybe

Ok ok I talk too much

I love it

You make me feel free

> I relate to that

To who the wine?

Kidding

>

Your pool boy has been working out

> Really?

Yup

Nic sends a pic of a weight machine at the gym. The pin for the weights is all the way down at the bottom of the stack.

Do you know what this is?

> It's the thing where you put the pin in and that's how much weight you lift?

Yeah on my favorite machine I'm all the way to the bottom now what do i do?

> Holy cricket
>
> I mean holy cricket

I want boobs like you

> Ha!

Christ

I know

> Then you won't need me

I want to taste you not just feel your boobs

Ok cut off

So sorry

> Keep going

I just want all of you

And you can have all of me

I'm not sure how much more naughty I'm supposed to be. Hard time reading the room 👀

I'm alone now

You mean we are alone now

I want to lick your pussy until you cum

Mmmmmm

Top to bottom

It won't take long because I'm really good at it. I take pride in it

Cheers 🥂

Careful you spilled some. Let me clean it up
👀😈💨❤️🍷

No doubt

I bet you taste amazing

I hope so

Soak my beard

Relax

Ok

Let me do my magic

Ok

I don't honestly think you would be able to handle that

I agree

Do you need a safe word just for me to go down on you?

Wait. I don't get it. What? Meaning a word to tell you to stop?

Yes silly

> Ok then

Some make safe words because of the pain aspect and I'm not about that. I'm about the pleasure side and sometimes it can feel so orgasmic that you can't take it anymore

> Yes Ok

You're going to cum more than you ever have. If I have permission of course

> You do

I just want you to be satisfied like you never have before

> Mmmmm sounds amazing

That's my job

Let me see you Babe

I send Nic a selfie while I sit on my balcony wearing a green sundress with my hair up. I'm half smiling.

Smile for Christ sakes

I was just between your legs. You could at least look half satisfied 🤦

> I hate taking pics of myself

It's just me Babe

I seen most of you 🤷‍♂️

> True
>
> I still don't like doing it

I have literally made you cum. Least you could do is send a pic ❤️🤷‍♂️

Low pressure silly

Wait til you hear my voice

> I can't wait

Wait til my lips kiss yours

> That's something I really can't wait for
>
> I think that's my favorite part
>
> Real kissing

I'm a very passionate kisser and feed off the other person to take it to the max if you want to

>

> You are a very passionate person

Take advantage of it please

Nic sends me a selfie of his face and bare chest showing.

> I will
>
> Hot

Hot for you, duh

>

You know you can flirt too?

> I don't?

Last time you flirted you were trying to give me mouth to mouth

Like 4:00 pm

🤣

I'm messing

> Oh ok
>
> I'm sorry

Don't be sorry I'm not being nice. I'm being a little frisky. So for that I'm sorry

> You are so sweet

Sometimes I get caught up in the moment

ONE HOUR GOES BY HERE

WYD

> I'm reading. I'm sorry I got too tired to text.

No worries luv
Enjoy

Tues, 22 Aug

12:09 am

Don't be awake

9:49 am

Morning

> Hi

Safe first word

 yep

Ty

You Alone?

Nope

You're lucky

I was about to send a pic

 Oh golly

Tues, 22 Aug

2:38 pm

WYD 👆

> Ok mister but you made fun of the safe greeting before you knew it was safe! Silly!

No one but us knows that is a greeting and would have no clue if they actually saw it

I'll do better sorry

I'm not used to being hidden usually women want to show me off

Totally messing. Trying to get you riled up.

> You always rile me up

If you want me to stop just say so

> I know

9:45 pm

You Alone?

> Yes

Nic sends me a pic of his bulging white underwear.

> That was from this morning I've been waiting for you to be alone 😉

Oh my goodness

> Sorry too far?

A little yes

> My bad

It's too risky for me to have pictures like that on my phone. I can't do that anymore. My phone isn't private enough.

> Oh I thought you said you delete our conversation
>
> I'm sorry

> I do. But the number of times they're communicating with Will using my phone was making me too nervous
>
> I'm sorry

No don't be sorry

I won't do that again unless you ask for it

> That's a good plan. Ty.

Tues, 22 Aug

> 8:11 pm
>
> Going to Cleveland tonight with my son to a Jazz jam.

Have fun Babe

>

If you think of me you can text me

>

Chapter 8
Focus – Lost and Regained

ONE WEEK GOES BY WITH NO COMMUNICATION

Mon, 28 Aug

8:58 pm

> Miss you.

Prove it

> I'm melting thinking about you

That's not proof

> I want to see you soon

Oh really

> I know I've been completely flighty
>
> And you don't have to put up with that

> You have some work to do

< Yes

> Are you ready to be a good little girl again?

< I think I'm a naughty little girl though

> Well why do you think that? You're so pure and innocent and untouched

< Because I've been so flighty to you and I don't mean to mistreat you

> It's ok you just lost your focus

< I did

< And life is completely totally 100% crazy and I know that's just not going to end anytime soon

< And it keeps getting crazier by the day

> It's ok that's why I am here for you to release and just have fun

You've been a big part of my support system

> I am your escape

Yes

I'm behind with my work and I'm running out of money. I'm missing Will like crazy. I just started a teaching job that's two days a week and I feel like I'm drowning already. So you were right. When you said it's not gonna get easier. I just have to get used to it.

> Just keep moving forward don't stay stagnant
>
> Things will get better. My life isn't easy either. But I need some kind of side attention
>
> To keep my mind sane

Yes

I know it's a bit far off, but can we plan to get together on September 9?

The next few weeks are completely packed for me

> Are you sure you're ready for that?

Yes!!!

> Do you deserve it?

I'm not sure I deserve it actually

You are like my mystery man

> I'm being totally playful right now not serious but this is hot
>
> So get back in the game
>
>

The world is so fucked up

> I'm not really trying to degrade you but it seems like this is a role for you. If I'm wrong say so

> I think you're right
>
> Thank you for being patient with me
>
> I was at a funeral today for a mom, my exact age. We have to enjoy life while we can.

Oh geez I'm sorry about the funeral

I'm only patient because I want to taste you so bad. That sweet preserved and reserved nectar. It's been so long for you and I want the first drop

> At least it puts life into perspective for the living

Live have some fun

> Yes
>
> And also today, my sister was on a campus with an active shooter

OMG where at?

Oh no

> I don't mean to be a downer I'm just trying to give you my state of mind
>
> She and her husband, and son were all on the same campus at the time in Georgia.

> The world is so fucked up and I just want to enjoy it while I still can
>
> And you have been so good to me

That's what I've been trying to get you to do

> Exactly

Your life is hard you should play hard too

Safe of course

> That is the best
>
> You always write the best text

Let me see you

> I'm having wine on my balcony right now

Thanks for the invite

>

I send Nic a selfie from my balcony. I'm wearing a blue V neck tank top and my head is tilted at a flirty angle and I'm smiling a big smile.

> I wish you could come here right now, but you're still a secret

> That's my baby girl

> Meet me at Edgewater Park 😊

> Oh my
>
> Love that idea
>
> I'm right across the street

> I know

> But I can't tonight

> Excuses
> Flirting

> That idea is making me hot though

> The gazebo in the garden

> Oooohhh yes
> The one that's behind the pond?

> They made those new docks just for us

> 😆😆😆

> And the fountain would be all lit up for us

> I could walk there to meet you
>
> Oh my

I know that's why I said it

> Hold on
>
> I had a picture of the fountain from my walk recently, but I can't find it
>
> I walk there a lot
>
> You're too awesome you deserve someone better than me

I'm just here to make you feel awesome too. That's my job

I send Nic a pic of my stemless wine glass a quarter filled with white wine. It's sitting on my balcony railing with another apartment building's lights glowing in the background.

> How did I deserve you?

> You don't yet. You still owe me

>> Yes
>>
>> Do you know when I just answer you with "Yes" it's like you've completely melted me and that's all I can say.
>>
>> Your words have the power to melt me

> Are you wanting to be submissive?

>> Yes
>>
>> Your words have so much power over me

> Ok I'll do that but nothing I say is meant negatively or truely derogatory and if I cross a line say so. I don't think I will but I want you safe

>> You are the best

> I know

>> Can you get together on September 9?

> We will see if you earn it by then

> I will tell you I don't have the kids that weekend

>> I want your hug and kiss so badly
>>
>> I don't want to disappoint you
>>
>> I don't want to be flighty any more

> You'll be fine just follow directions

>>
>>
>> Hmmmmmmm
>>
>> Does my behavior lead you to respect me or not?
>>
>> I've had a few glasses of wine, so I'm not sure what I'm writing. You are respectful btw

> What do I like you to do?

>> Omg I wish I could melt in your arms RN

> What do I like you to do?
>
> How submissive are you willing to be?

> I'm not sure
>
> I just want to make you happy
>
> You are so good to me

> Natalie how kinky do you want to be?

> Not very I think
>
> I'm happy with things not very kinky

> Ok tell me what you like and want to try
>
> Hot passionate sex is perfect. I just want to hear you say it Babe
>
> I want you to express your desires even how simple you think they are. Remember I like conservative panties. I'm not asking for much

> Hot passionate traditional sex would be ahhmazing
>
> Ahhhhmazing
>
> With french kissing
>
> I haven't had French kissing in years
>
> And that's what I crave the most

> That's beautiful because I am such a good sensual kisser. I bet I can make you cum just kissing you

I send Nic a pic from my balcony looking into my bedroom where Harris is sitting directly on top of my laptop keyboard.

> Y'all working hard over there

> Oh Babe it's gonna be a reality

That would be crazy wonderful. I've literally been teaching my cat to stay off my keyboard and he's literally sleeping on it right now

Mmmmmm

I'm so ready

> You'll be dripping wet before we even have intercourse

I'm sure!!!!!!

Did you like my picture of my wine glass in my view?

> That's a great view!

> You get me wet just with your texts

> Just imagine what my kisses, touch, tongue and fingers can do

> Mmmmmmmmmmmm
>
> I do have a great view
>
> Thanks to my parents

> You deserve it

> You are my awesome buddy and I'm so grateful for you

> I'm here for you

> I was just going to ask you how did I deserve you?
>
> I really can't wait to meet you
>
> These have been the most erotic and sexy exchanges I've ever had

> Boys start school yet?

They start tomorrow. I can't believe it

> What time?

7:20
What district are your kids in?

> Highland Square

Nice

> I'll be over at 7:30 be ready

😆😆😆😆

> What?

> You are rocking my world
>
> I'm so lucky to have you

I won't stay long just long enough to satisfy you

> Mmmmmmm
>
> Are you real?
>
> I'm thinking you're AI again
>
> Do you know which apartment I am?

The complex yes not the number

> I'm drunk RN
>
> Ooooh ok

Let me see you

> I could tell you

Let me see you

Nic sends selfie smiling with face and bare chest.

You could meet me at the park

I send him back a selfie. I'm smiling and sort of laughing on my balcony in the dark.

why do you look so happy?

I'm happy to be talking to you again

And that you haven't given up on me

Never gave up on you. Had a tough life changing thing. I get it. I'm patient

>

> I want to fulfill your fantasy

> Omg I could fall for you

> You just have to dig deep and tell me what it is when you're ready

> Yes
>
> Some night later we'll have to meet at Edgewater Park

> Promise?

> But I have you on my calendar for September 9
>
> Yes
>
> I'm not lying when I say, the next few weeks are completely completely crazy
>
> I have a ton of deadlines to meet before September 1

> And all weekend I'll be in Cleveland at the jazz festival every single day and night ♥

Yup I leave for Pittsburgh tomorrow for the week for work. Then kids this weekend

> Oh boy wow
>
> You're gonna have fun

Maybe

> 😂
>
> I'm definitely drunk at this point
>
> I'm going to go pee RN

Send me a cute pic

Not peeing

> I don't know what to send you

Whatever you feel is sexy and you're comfortable with

> I can't really do that
>
> It would just be the same as the one from a few minutes ago

That's ok. I live for the moment

I send him a similar selfie from my balcony in the dark wearing a black V neck shirt smiling again.

> My eyes can't stay open because the flash is so bright

Good girl

>

> I obey
>
> I can't wait to meet you

Is that what you want?

> Yes
> I want to
> Show you
> How much

Please do

> Appreciate you

How would you show me?

> By loving your body
> Like you deserve

Describe how I deserve it

> You deserve to be inside
> All the way inside if you want

In your sweet spot?

> Yes
> All the way in

> Nice and slow tho

>> Yes!!!!!
>> Even in public
>> You deserve it
>> I'll risk it

> You're making me hard

>> I need to show you I appreciate your friendship
>> Your loyalty has paid off

>> I haven't been easy
>> I want you

> You have not been easy and most would have walked away. You owe me more than you know

I send Nic a selfie showing my bare legs crossed with my feet up on the balcony railing. There are lights twinkling in the background from the other apartment building.

> Yes

> Now you're teasing that's not fair

> I love to tease you
>
> It makes us both happy
>
> And excited

> So soft and fresh shaved

> Yes
>
> I want you really badly
>
> You are a true friend
>
> A hot friend
>
> I'm so grateful for you

Nic sends me a selfie. He's wearing a blue tee shirt and smiling.

> You deserve to just relax and be free

>
>
> Can I say I love you without it being heavy??

Spell it Luv 😉

Oh ok.

I luv u

😂

Perfect

You ducking crack me up

And I don't mean Ducking I mean it with an F

I know

I want to fuck you now tho not make luv

Yes

Deep and hard

Yes

Please

All the way in slow and back out slow too

> I'm wet
>
> Yes yes

Your pussy lips are trying to pull my cock back in

> Exactly
>
> Yes
>
> They are

You are becoming wet

I can feel the build up

> I want u inside me
>
> Yes
>
> You turn me on so badly

Look at me when I'm fucking you

> Yes

> I want your eyes on me or in the back of your head
>
> Understood

> Yes yes I understand
>
> I want you
>
> I'm wet for you

> Now I'm gonna start hip thrusting

> My pussy is throbbing for you
>
> I need you

> Spread your legs wide to let me in deeper

> Yes

> Don't look away missy

> Ok

Don't lose focus like before

> Ok

Relax
Let me all the way in

> Ok I want you all the way deep in
> Please

Gonna stretch you open a little bit

> Yes
> But gently

Yes Of course

> Please
>
> Don't leave me waiting

My cock is throbbing RN

> Mmmmmmm
>
> You know how to get a girl Hot

Will you play with yourself while I'm in there. I'll go slow

> Yes
>
> I just want you
>
> In me
>
> You make me so hot
>
> Like no one else

I'm gonna push down gently on your inner thighs with my hands to change position and get in even deeper

> I need to kiss you

> Feet up in the air
> Just relax

>> Yes ok
>> Please please

> Relax your pussy

>> I'm ready
>> Ok
>> It is

> Just let the juices flow

>> I want you

> All over my cock

> My panties are wet

And that sound starts happening. Just total release and air flow collaborating

> Yes yes omg

You know

> Yes

And that's when your eyes go into the back of your head

And you just let me take total control

> I'm open for you.
> Yes

I want you to cum one more time

> Yes

Now I'm going fast I want the heat

> I want you

The friction

> Yes
> I want you

Relax and moan if you need to

> Ok I do need to
> I want you

You can have me

> How can we be this hot for each other?

Cause you make me hot

> And you me

Did you cum again?

> I can't wait to meet you
> I didn't touch myself that time
> I just let the momentum build

Did you cum?

> I'm very wet

Want me to keep going?

> I guess not. This is perfectly hot the way it was

I want to fuck you on your patio RN

> Should we ever meet at the park or is that a bad idea?

Can you be quiet?

> I can be
>
> I want you
>
> I want to straddle you

Then we can meet at the park or fuck on your patio.

But I've got to be honest I don't think you're going to be able to be quiet. You've never been with a Viking before

> Oooohhh my
>
> We can't be on my patio because everyone would see

Let them see what a good girl you are

> Oh my

You said you wanted to in public

> Yes
>
> Do the police roam the park?

Babe there are trails too

There's this hot archway of vines we could fuck in there

> But what would the bottom be like?
>
> Ouchy?

Bend over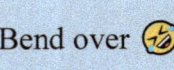

But I need you on top of me or me straddling you while you're sitting

You can straddle me there I'll bring a blanket

Ok

Fuck my brains out

Yes

If you even could

I know right

I want you

Really bad

> Ok silly I'm trying to get you to say that you would fuck my brains out
>
> Threaten me a little bit

Yes

> Lol

What should I say?

I need you inside me

Can you do that?

> Use a finger with me?

How?

> Which hand do you prefer

Right

> Well I'm left handed but use your right middle finger and just play a little
>
> Do you write with your right hand?

Yes

> Use your left and pretend it's mine

Ok

I'm melting now

> Just touching the outside
>
> Seeing boundaries
>
> And softness

Mmmmmmm

> Take a sip of wine

Cat is fully asleep on laptop

I'm out of wine

For tonight

> Ok well my finger is ready to explore
> Permission?

< I still feel it
< Yes yes yes
< I want you
< Please
< Remember I luv u

> Put that finger ALL the way in one time

< Ok
< I just need you

< Now

> Is it in?

< Yes

> Slowly back out

> It's too much

Are you tight like Daddy likes it?

> Yes
>
> Please come inside me

Can I fill you up?

> Yes
>
> Please
>
> I'm yours

Play with your clit as I start to cum

> Ok

I'm gonna have to go jack off now because of you

> Yes

I'm fully loaded

Good

I pre cum

In my shorts

I'm soaking wet

I'm like a slip and slide

Soaking wet granny panties 😉 ❤️ ❤️

Yes

What's more conservative you or your panties?

Panties

Mmmmmmmm

> Mmmm

> I want to snuggle them

> Yeah
> My hand is on my pussy, pretending it's you

> Put your finger in. Any one of 'em
> Which one did you pick?

> Middle, right

> Is it deep?

> You're touching me

> Do a circular motion
> Open it up a bit

> More

> Just relax

My pussy's wanting you

> Would two fingers fit?
>
> Slowly

Yea

I want your cock

Slow

> Put another finger in and then you may feel kinda what it's gonna be like

Mmmmm

> Ring finger

Was I late for school?

> I didn't want to bring it up but yes

> Am I being punished?

You can pay that debt on September 9th if you're lucky

This is just for you losing focus

> Mmmm

Are you focused?

> Yes

Get both those fingers in there deep

> Ok

You better be wet

> I am sir
>
> I'm in your office because I was late for school

Good that's what it feels like to have my cock buried in you. Full and wet

> Yea

Do you like your hair pulled? Not hard just firm grasp

> I don't know
>
> Your hand is on my pussy because I was late for school

Bad girl

> And I can't leave until I come

Now I'm gonna have to make you suffer

My two fingers are tightly pressed together my other two fingers are at a 90 degree angle so the two longest and thickest fingers can get in deep

You ever watch a sewing machine?

> Yes. I'll never be late again I promise

You ever see a sewing machine?

> Yes

> How fast the needle comes up and down?

>> Yes
>>
>> My pussy is being tortured by your cock

> So fast so fast it is going in and out

>> Yeah

> And then I stop with both fingers buried in you
>
> Plugged up
>
> And I pulsate my two fingers slowly

>> Yes
>>
>> Slow
>>
>> I am wide open for my punishment

> Yes and this makes you very wet and you build up again. I can feel your muscles twitching

>> You can give it to me now, please

> Let me just put my cock in please
>
> Just the tip
>
> Please

> Please

> Did you just look away?

> Yes

> Bad girl

> Please come inside me

> Ow I'm gonna fuck you on my terms
>
> Now

> Yea

> Hold on tight

Ok

> Relax that pussy and those hips
>
> I'm not playing around

Ok

> Moan damnit

If u say so

Mmmmmmmm

> Do you like gentle pressure applied to your neck while fucking

Maybe

I'm wide open

> Just gentle
>
> So you know I mean business

Ok

> I want you to cum on my cock now
>
> You been bad

I'm soaking

Yes

I need to

> You want me to fill you up again?

Yes

> You've been bad
>
> So I'm gonna pull out and you can take it in your mouth or on your tits. That's your choice

> I'm rocking on your cock
>
> Mmmmm

You gonna take it all in the mouth

> Stick it
>
> Inside me

In your mouth?

> In my pussy

Nope you have been bad. You don't deserve it

> It's aching for you

Do you think three fingers would fit? Will that do the trick?

> I want your cock
> Inside

You haven't earned it yet

> Please
> Give it to me anyway
> I need you inside

So you want me to fuck you

> Yes
> Please

Meet me at the park

> I want to

> I won't send it but I wish you could see how wet my shorts are

>> I want you
>>
>> You see everything

> I still think you're too innocent

>> I mean you are everything
>>
>> That's ok
>>
>> What if that section of the park is closed off?

> It would be ours

>> It was the other day when I was walking

> We own that section

>> Mmmmmm

> Let me own you in that gazebo
>
> You're mine right?

> The one behind the pond?
>
> Yes I am

> In the major garden
>
> Iron fencing
>
> All mine

> Behind the iron fencing?

> Yes closest to the building

> Ok. I think I know.
>
> We can't tonight though
>
> Tomorrow's the first day of school

> I know silly. I'm way too intoxicated to drive and you wouldn't make it past your bed
>

> I'm still role playing

> > I know.

> You need to go to bed

> > It's so exciting
> >
> > I do need to
> >
> > Must wake up to see the seniors off
> >
> > 5:45 am

> I leave for Pittsburgh @ 7:00 am

> > How fun this was
> >
> > You'll be there for the week?

> Yes for the week

> > Wow

I have a student acting up down there

Kidding

Uh oh

Oh good

You have a student acting up up here

It's our company work meeting

She's doing a little better now that she has come to her senses

No Pittsburgh hookers

I want some sexy pics before the 9th

No hookers geez

Ok but they'll be fully dressed sexy pics

You know what I like

If you don't do your homework by the time I see you, you will be punished again

OK sir

I promise

I'll do what you say

As you should

Omg

That's what good little girls do, you know

> You melt me
>
> Have a great trip
>
> I wish I could sneak into your hotel room

Maybe you can be a distraction for me at night time while I'm all alone in my hotel room

> Yes
>
> Hopefully

Since you still owe me

> I do

Sweet dreams

By the way, when we meet a the park we'll be almost fully clothed except for a few key areas

So if anyone finds us, it won't look like what it is

> Hey I'll follow your lead, You seem to be a pro

>
> Luv u

LUV you too ❤️🔥😗

>
> Drive safe

I'm not driving. We are carpooling 👤

> Nice
>
> Tell your driver to drive safe from me
>
>
>
> Night night

I will

Sweet dreams

> You too
> ❤️

Chapter 9
It's Getting Hard To Type

Tues 29 Aug

5:46 am

GM

I'm on my way over

Mmmmmm

They JUST left

Get your little skirt on Daddy's coming to play

How you feeling?

Little hung over otherwise good

How about you?

I think I need a nap now before I start the day

Let me help put you to sleep

How?

Let me see you

Nic sends me a selfie. He's wearing a blue tee shirt and smiling.

I'm too asleep to take a picture

I'm sorry

I'll remember how disobedient you were

Tues 29 Aug

2:45 pm

I send him a selfie standing on my balcony with a blue sleeveless top and gold necklace on. My hair is curly and I'm giving a big, smirky smile.

> I owed u this one

> Good girl

>

Tues 29 Aug

8:53 pm

> Hey

> One word safe

> Yes! Good job. I basically just got my phone back from my son who left his at his friend's house.

> I follow the rules don't I?
> Nicely

> Yes you do

How come you don't do the same?

>
> Your texts are the best. I know I always say that but it's true

I'm so lonely here

> I'm sorry
>
> Aren't hotels fun though?

Not when it's all people in the same company plus HR is here. So no, not fun

> Oh boo

That's why I want your attention

> Ok
>
> You got it

Even tho I'm hundreds of miles away

I could find some Pittsburgh hooker or change my Tinder location and find something local

But I want you

> You're on Tinder???

Loosely. I hate it

Too many fakes

> Well I'm not fake

How do I know?

> Hhhhmmmmmm good question
>
> Sometimes I think ur AI because ur texts always hit me right where it counts
>
> So we each think the other is fake

I'll just prove who I am on the 9th 🔥

🔥🔥
I'm so excited

Show me

How?

I'm making dinner for boys

No worries. Be chef for awhile and check back when you can

Ok

10:38 pm

Hey

Yes

Can I help you, late night surfer?

WYD

Getting ready for bed with my kitty

> I want to go to bed with kitty

> Last night was so fun
>
> I got a little tipsy talking with u

> I want more
>
> I know. It's ok it's just me you're talking to

> I know
>
> Are you in bed yet?

He sends me a selfie of his legs, wearing shorts and socks and laying on a hotel bed with a white bedspread under him.

> Waiting for you

> Awwww
>
> Anything good on TV?

I'd rather have your attention and a pic of you than TV

> You have my attention

Let me kiss you all over

> Yes please
>
> I want your kisses

Do I have permission to kiss anywhere?

> Yes

Mmmmmmm

> Anywhere and everywhere

Are you sure?

> 100%

You're making me hard

> I wish I could climb on top of you RN

Go ahead

I want you to take control tonight

> I want to get on top and rub my pussy all over your hard cock but not put it all the way in

> I love that
>
> Just okay with it on the outside?

Yes

> Look at me when you're doing that tho

Yes

I'm looking at you and rubbing up and down

Slowly

> I want to grab your hips

Yes

> And just feel you taking charge

> Yes

> Relax

> Ok
> But now I need you inside
> I need the tease to end
> Can you come inside me now?

> Babe it's early

> Please

> Are you ready to be filled up?

> Yes

Show me what I like

> I'm soaking wet for u
> I'm all opened up for you

Show me you

> I can't do late night pics I'm sorry

Why? You are so sexy. It's just me

> I'm sorry

No need to be sorry

You just make me so hot and racy

With your conservativeness

> You are hot
>
> With your perfect chest hair

I'm not wanting to see your pussy. Just something to help my mind wander

> I know but I can't take pics like that when I'm in bed

So disobedient

I'm gonna have to take this into consideration for a punishment

> Omg I want you inside me so badly RN

And I want a sexy pic

> I can't do it Babe

> Just give in to me
>
> Relax
>
> You'll finally feel what you want

I want you to slip yourself inside me

> So get what you want

You don't want that?

> I want you to fucking moan loud then

Are you mad at me?

> No silly. Why?

Because I can't give you a pic

> I'm sorry maybe I'm reading this too sexually in a role
>
> Babe it's ok. I never want you to do anything you don't feel comfortable doing
>
> But you better make it up somehow
>
> Understood?

Yes sir

> Straddle me

I want you

Yes

> Are you facing me?

Yes

I'm grinding on you

And feeling your strong tight chest

> It's a nice chest

>> I love how it looks
>> I can't wait to talk to you in person

> Are you going to be able to handle it?

>> I'm not sure
>> It just may be too much for me

> Do I need security?

>> Yes!!
>> Have them on stand by

> I want you to like you say straddle me. But I want you to control the flow

> I'd love to
>
> Slow then fast

Look at me and tell me with your eyes you want control so I know to just relax and get into place for you

> Omg that's so hot

Give me your palms and just fuck me the way you want to. The way you want to feel it

> It's getting hard to type
>
> You have me on fire

Babe you're in control

You have me hard AF

Keep going

> I need you now
>
> Slowly in and out but when it's in it's in deep
>
> Over and over again

And pause for a second when it's all the way in

And pause on the out

> Yes
>
> That's perfect
>
> And I want your lips on mine at the same time

Of course and simple French kissing

> And you can feel the muscles of my pussy gripping you tighter and letting go and then tighter again
>
> I'm so wet I can smell it

Can you use your muscle like that?

> I think so

> I want your eyes locked into mine if you do that. I want to know that you are meaning to do that not just feel it

Yes

> Cum on my cock please
>
> I want to feel it and hear it

Yes

> Harder
>
> And I shouldn't be saying this since you're in control

I want you to go down on me

> Yes ma'am
>
> I'd love to

> Lick

Top to bottom

With a flat tongue

Top

You're being kinda sassy eh?

> My finger is your tongue

Slowly then

Round and round

> Yes

Then I'll play with your clit

> Y

I'm worried for you

> Then crawl up me and kiss me more
>
> Then I need you inside of me all the way with your hardness
>
> I need to cum

My cock is so hard

> Can I cum now?

Throbbing

> Mmmmm

Far away from home all alone

And all I want is YOU

> Oooohhhhhhh

I want to fuck you and make you feel naughty

> Yes

I don't want you to back out if this is too hot

> I won't

What if you keep cumming and cumming and can't stop but you want me to stop?

> I won't

Can I cum now then?

Yes

But what if I'm not ready?

I don't know

Let me put it in your mouth

Ok

If you don't like it then say so. I don't want to do anything you are not into

> I think it's ok as long as no STD

Babe seriously

I am clean

> Ok. Me too.
>
> You never know. It seems like you have a lot of sex though

I know I talk a lot of flirt but not a lot of actions if you know what I mean

> Yes I do
>
> Ok

I'm not as sexually active as I talk. It's fantasy for me.

> Ok
>
> I see

> And if I never meet you then even more safe

>> I want to meet you

> I talk with you differently than any other woman. Not that there are a lot but you hold a special place in my heart

>> Thank you ❤

> For what?

>> That I hold a special place in your heart

> No. You earned that so that's not a thank you necessarily
>
> I want to taste you

> Yes
>
> I'm almost cumming

My tongue will send you over the moon

I promise

> Please
>
> I'm on top again

Lock your hips in

Get in place

> Yes

Do your thing Babe get after it

> I just came
>
> Omg Babe
>
> Thank you for that
>
> Mmmmmm
>
> We're going to be so good together

That's my job Babe

Did you cum tonight?

I won't lie to you. No

It's ok. I enjoyed this too

Ok well I'm glad you liked it

You can make it up to me

Ok

Luv u

I fucking luv you too!

I want to just destroy you RN

In a good way

You are so fun

I can't take it

Want me to stop?

No but I have to stop soon

I want to cum

What can I do

To help you?

Tell me you're in control

Just simply do that

> I am in control. I'm on top of you. You do as I say.

Mmmmm

Yes Momma

> You are at my mercy

Take me

> We're going at my speed
>
> I'm looking into your eyes

Mmmm

> You're deep inside me like I like it
>
> Do you like it?

> I want you to keep control

> I'm going up and down on you with you inside me

> Palms touching

> You're just sitting there
>
> Yes palms touching

> Feeling you

> We're hot and sweaty

> Don't stop

> We're doing things my way

Yes boss

> You have no control

I'm at your mercy

> I'm dictating

Have your way

> Up and down
>
> Your dick is all mine
>
> It's for my pleasure

> I'm all in for your desire
>
> Do what you want with me

I'm sliding down to suck your dick for a minute

> Mmmmm

You just sit there

> You are great at that

And enjoy

> I can't even sit still

> And you get to receive

Take me to climax
Can you?

> I don't know if I can
> I can with you in my pussy
> Is that ok?

Keep trying
It feels good with your lips around my cock

> I will try
> I'm kissing your cock

Mmmm

> It's inside my mouth

> You know what you are doing quit playing it off

I'm licking it all around

And I have to move my hair out of the way

> If you actually did that it would make me cum instantly

The licking?

> Yes

Ahhhhh

I'm licking even more

> Sorry it would be a mess

> Did you make a mess yet tonight?

Almost

I'll save it for you tho

Let me fill you up

>
> Yes

Dripping wet

> Yes
> So I'd have to take a shower

Sweet dreams

> You too

> You have me hot and bothered
>
> I'm gonna jack off now

Go for it Babe

> Will you swallow?

Nope

Sorry

> No it's okay then I know what to do with it

You'll have to give me a warning

So I know it's coming

> What if I just leave it in and you actually enjoy it?

> No thank you

Can I cum on your face, tits, lower back?

> Not face please

>

Go to bed or I'm going to fuck your brains out FRFR and you won't be able to walk tomorrow

> FRFR?

> For real for real
>
> Lol

That's what I thought

Night night

> Sweet dreams

You too

---- Wed, 30 Aug ----

7:41 pm

> Hey

Hey

> Let me see you

I send Nic a pic of my sad face.

> You caught me crying

> Awe. Why Babe?

> Will just called mad at me bc I'm 'wasting hundreds of thousands of dollars' since I got a new lawyer
>
> My ex is telling him stuff

> So in my decree we wrote we cannot talk about each other to the kids.
>
> You need to document this stuff

> We have that too
>
> He doesn't care

> When is the divorce final?

> Early December if we can agree on everything by then
>
> I don't have time for his shit. I have all these deadlines to meet by end of August
>
> I'm sorry to dump on you
>
> You reached out right when I needed u ♥
>
> You've done that before

> I'm here for you

> Thank you

> Oh you will

Won't you?

♥♥

Awe so shy you can't even answer

I will thank you. Don't worry.

Awe Babe I know. I'm messing

I know

How was today?

I've had a cocktail

Today was boring

> Ahhh. Sorry about it being boring
>
> What cocktail did u have?

Well 3 beers for now. Now I think I'm gonna get ice cream. They gave us a gift card for an ice cream place next door

> Fun!!
>
> What's your go to flavor?

I'm a chocolate shake kinda guy

> Yum

Wed 30 Aug

11:39 pm

Park?

You're home?

No

That was my one word in

Lol

That was a good one

WYD

If I was back home you would have known

First hand 😉

I'm going to bed now

> Sweet dreams
>
> Let me tuck you in tho

Ok

> Nah. I'll definitely cross the line. Sweet dreams Babe

Night night

Nic sends me a smiling selfie.

Awwww cutie

Chapter 10
Do We Have to Wait Any Longer?

Wed 31 Aug

7:23 am

GM

Let me see you

I send him a selife while I'm laying in bed, my hair is messed up, I'm giving a smirky smile, Harris the kitty is on my chest. The angle of the pic makes my boobs look extra big.

Wow

You caught me at a good time

They are so big

Sorry

 There is some distortion in that picture

Cats in the way

And the shirt

 This camera really distorts pictures depending on the angle

Can I play with them some day?

Yes please

> Good girl

I send him a pic taken from my bedroom looking out onto my balcony. The early morning light make the entire scene glow a golden color.

< I love the view from my bed

> Mmmmmmm
>
> Wish I was snuggling you

< Me too

> Do you have pants on?

< Yes

Oh

But I have to shower in a few minutes

Take me with you

Don't be shy

Daddy deserves it

I took a job teaching two days a week

I'm hot for teacher

I've never fucked a teacher before

Maybe I deserve detention

Ooooohhh me either

But you're my principal remember

I have my own office

Yes you do sir

Desk

And the door closes

> We need to talk

> I'm scared to talk unless we're in person

> No I mean the door closes and that's what I say

> Oh yes

> I know I'm your boss but I can't keep my eyes off of you

>

> And your conservative outfits got me on fire
>
> I have to taste you

> Yes
>
> Please

You're the only teacher for me

>
>
> But you have to discipline me because I was late for school

I'll hike your skirt up and use my ruler to spank you

>
>
> But then you have to lay me down on the desk

My office my rules

Then I may lay you down on the desk

I promise never to be late again

I'll see you tomorrow same place same time

Late every day on purpose

I'll try really hard not to be late but it's hard

Aren't you sick of my cock?

No, I'm not

Oh it's hard

I'd show you but I'm in the car with 3 people. And you don't like to see those I know

> Oh my goodness you're naughty right now
>
> I'm laying on my bed touching myself thinking it's you

Natalie I'm always naughty

Keep going

>

I want you to cum

Don't disappoint Daddy

Faster

> K

Relax

Cum for me

> K

> I want to stuff my cock all the way in

> > Yes

> I'm so hard RN

> > Mm
> > I want you to make me cum

> I want to make you squirt

> > I mean I want you inside

> Ok Babe I'm about to walk into meetings. Finish for me. Take me with you.
>
> Send me pics if you feel sexy

> K
>
> I'll meet you in the bathroom in the middle of your meetings and we'll do it on the sink

No one will hear you because it's so loud. We are at Dave and Busters

Moan as loud as you want

> Oh my God yes
>
> Have a great day

You too. Enjoy the shower

I can talk for 8 minutes

Make it worth Daddy's time

> I'm still touching myself wanting U

How many fingers

> One

> All the way in and leave them there. Pause

> I can't come by myself very easily

> That's why I'm here Babe

> Yes

> Let me take the pressure off of you

> But you're not in the bedroom with me

> Excuse me?

> You're not here with me

I am missy

Don't talk back

>

> I luv u
>
> You're the fucking best

I'll show you how to LUV properly if you would just relax and be a little promiscuous

Just let go of your conservative side a little, that's all I'm asking. Have fun.

> Ok

> Show me vulnerability 😉
>
> You know you want to

>> I'm not good at doing that
>>
>> Yes I want to

> Babe you would be perfect for it
>
> Acting all shy
>
> You know you want to be a Cougar and pounce this cougar bait

>> Yes

> Am I wrong?

>> No

> All we have been through who better to just let loose with and show your naughty side to?

> No one

> I'll leave it in your hands when you're ready
>
> I'll let you tell me when you're ready to take that step
>
> Ok, meeting is starting. Finish for me in the shower. Chat soon.

> You did it. I came.
>
> Thank you my darling
>
>

> That's my job Babe

Thur 01 Sep

3:52 pm

Hey

Hey. I'm driving right now so I can't really talk

Ok no worries just saying hi

Thur 01 Sep

6:33 pm

Hey I'm about to go underground until probably Tuesday. It's the perfect storm coming up. I have many deadlines to meet for Tuesday but then I have to be at the Jazz Festival a lot of the time.

Hopefully I can say hi to you now and then. Don't worry I'll be back around at the beginning of next week.

Ok

Check in when you can

Luv ya

> Luv you too

> Your Daddy will be patiently waiting

>
>

>

> I mean after I get through these four crazy days you mean?

> Just a little more naughty like we talked about you wanting to try. Low pressure, I'm egging you on

> Ok
> Here's a pic I took for you earlier today, but didn't send.

The selfie I send him shows me kneeling on the floor wearing jeans, a black shirt and a long gold necklace. My hair is pulled back and I have a closed mouth smile.

you on your knees

Yep

Good girl

You are so hot

How do you do it?

I'll show you one day

But you have to be really good and get all your work done before I show you anything

Yep. I will. It's gonna suck, but I will

> I'll make the wait worth it I promise

< Just a head's up, my son will be getting in the car in a few minutes

> Ok chat when you can

< Ok

Fri 01 Sep

11:43 pm

< Just saying hi and good night

> GN I'm up if you want more

> I just want to say hi more but not have sex
>
> When do you come back?

I'm home silly

> Oh you're home already?
>
> Nice

WYD

> I'm still writing

You don't have to answer me if you are needing to be working

Ok. Thank you. Thank you for letting me check in. I am still writing. I had another client from the past reach out to me today. The clients are coming like gangbusters all of a sudden. I guess that's what happens when you take a part time job for money because of a lack of clients. Then the clients just come rushing in.

Yup. Murphy's Law

You got this.
I believe in you

Chat later

 thanks

Fri 01 Sep

I send him a selfie from my couch wearing a white V neck tee shirt with my hair pulled back and my glasses on. Harris the kitty is on the back of the couch behind me.

> Fri 01 Sep

11:08 am

> Just wanted to say hi and say that I handed in an email to a client last night from the jazz festival and he said he only had to change one word! So excited. We're back at the jazz festival today and I'm at a pizza place doing my writing until later. I hope you're good.

4:32 pm

What's up

> I just wanted to chat with you and you weren't responding
>
> I know I'm super busy and I'm not trying to mess with you. I just wanted to say hi cause I'm working my brains out

> You told me you were going to need me to give you space so you could work. Even tho you are reaching out to me I'm trying to avoid talking so you can get back to work. I know how sidetracked I can make you. I'm not meaning to be distant but respectful of your wishes.

You are so good

Thank you

This weekend just really sucks and I just want to say hi for a second

You do make me sidetracked for sure

But you kind of do even when we're not texting and you can't help that that's just my brain going towards you

And yesterday was super emotional and I would just love a Nic hug

> Absolutely

> Luv hugging you

> Thank youuuuuu

> Now get back to work Daddy said so
>
> Insert stern voice

>
> Ok. I am.
>

I send Nic a selfie with my hair pulled back and eye glasses on again. But this time I'm wearing a green V neck tee shirt and I'm smiling with no teeth. I'm sitting in a pizza place.

Impressive you almost sent cleavage 🤣😈❤️

Sat 02 Sep

11:26 pm

Hey

We're about to go to The Velvet Tango Room so Daniel can jam with some of these jazz musicians 😃

Awesome

So cool

Edgewater Monday PM 😉

😆

Just an option you don't even have to comment

🔥
This place is hopping

Enjoy the atmosphere

I send Nic a selfie from the Velvet Tango Room. My hair is pulled back in a low ponytail. I'm giving a shy smile and wearing a black shimmery sleeveless top, and there is a grainy golden-lit vibe surrounding me.

> Thanks

How can you just send me that and not want me to make you mmmmmmm

Is that a cocktail dress?

> No it's not. I'm wearing jeans
>
> But my top is sparkly

I notices 😉

> Very perceptive

> I know what I want and see what is there

Hi Babe

I send him a picture showing my red-painted nails holding a long-stem wine glass filled with white wine. My jean-clad legs are crossed and one open-toe sandaled foot is dangling above the bar floor.

Sorry I don't mean to tease you. Just wish you were here to flirt with tonight

Sun 03 Sep

2:23 am

Night night

5:44 am

12:30 pm

Today I'm doing my work at the hotel restaurant where the jazz fest is

Nice.

With my 2 glasses of wine last night hangover 😆

You should have called me for the rescue! 🤣

Rescue me from the wine?

Or take advantage of you because of it

Get back to work little missy

Ok I know. Ugh.

Daddy will be waiting here when you are finished.

I have a nice surprise for you

Now I need to know the surprise…

You don't need to talk back to Daddy 😉

Get your work done and be on time

> You're right. Ok.

Don't you forget that. Write that shit down in sharpie

> Ok.

I send him a screenshot of a Google Doc with the headline: Reignite Your Inner Spark–Boost Your Libido, Sexual Energy and Pleasure by 348% Even if You're Over 49 in just Weeks.

> This is the ad I'm working on today
>
> Don't worry, I don't need this product.

I am that product. That's the surprise

Sun 03 Sep

4:21 pm

I send Nic a selfie while I'm sitting on a lawn chair with a river and tons of people in the background. I'm wearing a black V neck sleeveless sundress. I smile with closed lips.

Taking a break listening to jazz

Look at that view 😉

Edgewater 8:30

I found another place today

Where

At the park?

No River Styx Cider Mill

Nice

Even better

They made this picnic area and cut down to the river. It's pretty sexy but I'm sure there are cameras it's close to the main building

So we can just hold hands and kiss there

But further down the path maybe could get a little interesting

I'll bring the bug spray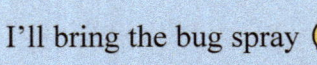

Don't want that delicate skin gettin' bit

Well not from bugs anyway 👀

Are you working?

Don't lie

Yep

That's not convincing

Get back to work.

> I just changed locations from outside by the water to back to the hotel
>
> Now I can charge my computer

Are you in your room or a public place?

> In the lobby, we did not get hotel rooms this weekend we've been driving back and forth

I send him a selfie from the hotel bathroom. In the pic, I'm standing in front of a floor to ceiling mirror wearing a black mini sundress and black sandals.

Yes please

All of you for the first time

> Let me press you against that mirror and do bad things

> What hotel? I'm on my way

> Crowne Plaza at Playhouse Square

> I've stayed there twice
> Overlooking the river

> Yep

> Always wanted to fuck someone while looking out the window but no luck

What?

I was with my kids for a wedding and stayed there

You didn't get to do that

Maybe you could be the one?

I'd love to

You gotta earn those kind of nights 😉

I will!

> That's what they all say

>> I'm not like them all

> Are you being assertive?

>> Yes. I'm your #1 girl

> That's a bold claim are you ready for that?
> I'm needy AF

>> I'm ready

> Not til the 9th

> That's right
>
> That's our night

Do you have conservative panties on under that conservative dress?

> Yes I do

Easy access tho

> Yep

For me or you

> Ok so Edgewater later?

Sun 03 Sep

10:19 pm

> I finished all those deadlines! So now I get to watch Daniel jam at The Velvet Tango Room for the next six hours 😁

> Ok so Edgewater later? Damn
>
> Late night

> This will be the third night of getting home at 3 am
>
> That's why (plus my deadlines) are why I said I'd be going underground until Monday / Tuesday

12:10 am

Hey

Hey

I'm so hot for you RN. You stood me up at the park 🤣 😈 🐿️

Ooops

I didn't know I did that

You were late. Well you didn't show the fuck up so punishment is coming

Ok

Wait are you brushing me off lol

> Just listening to jazz. My son is on stage

Oh snap. Then focus on him. Chat later LMK how it went

> Ok Luv

Tues 05 Sep

10:19 am

Hey

> Hey Babe

You Alone?

> No. Still at the bar
> Jam still going on

> Other guys hitting on you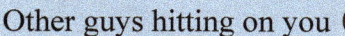

> !!

> Get it girl
>
> Can I share a pic?

> If it's pg rated

Nic sends me a selfie from his livingroom chair. He's wearing a black tee shirt and smiling.

> Hi!!

> Babe I know the rules I'm not trying to be weird with you

> Ok ok thank you

I'll never send you a dick pic unless you ask. It's not my motive. But if you want it I'll listen and oblige

Understood?

>
> Yes

I'm hot for you

>

> Awwwww
>
> I'm glad

I'm really being naughty RN

Or well my mind is

😆 You got yourself all worked up over there 😄

I blame you

What did I do? Aren't I innocent tonight?

We can talk about the bathroom pic of the full view ❤️❤️❤️ yeah that pic did it for me 😉 😋 💋

😄😄😄😄
Yay!
That makes me happy

I want you pressed against that glass and let me feel your body up and down

> Hmmmmm

> You can say no

> I want to say yes

> Good girl

> Is that what you like?

> Yes

> I know. I pay attention that's why I said it
> ❤️ 🦋

> You do

> I don't see a question mark so I guess that's a statement

> Yes

> Do you want more of it?

> I can't now Babe

> Oh lol. Ok no worries

> ❤️❤️

> Chat soon

Thanks

Mon 04 Sep

12:01 pm

> Hey

I send him a selfie from that same hotel bathroom mirror again. The pic shows my full body wearing a lacey tank top with a khaki mini skirt and black sandals on. My hair is pulled back in a low pony. There is a lot of gold trim on the walls in the background of the pic.

> Baby girl all dressed up
>
> Mmmmmm

Let me guess no panties

Nooooo not the case

I know silly. I'm sure there is 1000 thread count panties under there

😆

Tues 05 Sep

10:19 am

Hey

Hey

> You good?

Driving home now

> Ok chat later
>
> Or Edgewater you tell me

I can't do either tonight. I'm walking dead.

I'm sorry

> No worries Babe
>
> Be safe
>
> I was kidding about the park

Ok Ok 😆

Mon 04 Sep

10:19 pm

Hey

> Hey Nic 🧡🧡

WYD baby girl?

> I love when you call me that
>
> I'm going to see if I need new brakes

Then what?

> I have work to do after that. What are you up to?

I'm off today

About to go to the gym

> Oh nice I worked out at home this morning

I bet you got all sweaty

> I did 😁

Did you shower?

> Yes

Did you think of me?

> Yes I did

Did you touch?

Only for a second

Probably all it took 😉

Ok I'm going to the gym you're making me hard

It's so easy tho 😁

Yes because you drive me nuts sexually

I just don't like to rub one off then try to workout 👀

> You drive me nuts too

Do we have to wait any longer?

> I'm not sure. I really want to meet Saturday even tho it's hard to wait. It's not too much longer
>
> I don't want to tease you and I don't mean to
>
> Would it help if we didn't chat much this week and got back in touch Friday or Saturday?

Nah I'm messing

Don't get me wrong I want you NOW but I can wait

> Ok. Thank you. You are all I'm looking forward to

Chapter 11
Are You Sure You're Ready?

Tues 05 Sep

9:01 pm

Hey

Hi

WYD

Putting dishes away

Good girl

I didn't know it was possible to ruin a frozen dinner but I managed

It was ruined before you touched it

How did you manage that?

Let me explain. I put three TGI Friday's potato skins in the oven but didn't time it. Took them out too early. Then finished in the microwave but then they lost the crispiness.

Yup that will do it

I bet you still looked cute doing it

I can see your panic face

And then you say fuck it, choke it down boys

Can I see you?

I mean a pic

No. Not right now. I'm choking down potato skins 😁

Get used to it you'll be choking down something on Saturday

Sorry too far

Yes. That's ok.

Are you sure?

No

I walked for an hour at Edgewater tonight and thought of you ❤️❤️

Did you go to the east on the dirt path?

> I didn't go on a dirt path bc of bugs
>
> Just around the pond

So the main garden

With gazebo?

> Yes

Odd I didn't get invited ♥

>
> Next time

Tomorrow?

>

10:00 tonight

>
> I'll be in the shower then

Just for a kiss

Oh shower eh?

> One kiss will be impossible

I know

Who's gonna kiss first?

Isn't it mutual?

I'm bad at first moves

I'll wait and see how long it takes you

You will still be a Virgin

I expect a nice shower pic. You know I'm not asking for nudes but nice, naughty Natalie pics

You know what Daddy likes

10:49 pm

Hey

Just took an emergency trip to Walmart with my son for school supplies. Now I'm taking a shower 😁

Prove it

I just got out

And…..

You are so hot I can not wait to see you in person

I worked out extra hard for you today

So excited to feel those muscles

Chest and triceps mainly

Mmmmm

Perfect

Will you put your hands on my chest when you are riding me

Yes I will

Then you will see the work I've been doing 😊

Nic sends me a selfie. He's showing a smiling face and the upper part of his bare chest.

> Hi cutie

Sweet dreams

> You too

I'm not going to bed. But I am saying goodnight because I won't be able to contain myself if we keep chatting tonight

I want you soooo bad

> Yes same. I think it's best to say goodnight now. Plus my entire weekend was going to bed at 3 am and I'm a zombie at this point 😢

Sweet dreams. I want to be in them

> I bet you will be. I'll let you know tomorrow

Mmmmmm

Wed 06 Sep

2:12 pm

I send him a pic of Harris lounging on a grey fluffy blanket winking at the camera.

A wink for you from Harris

He's thrilled

Let me see you baby girl

I send Nic a selfie wearing a green sleeveless mini dress. My hair is down and curly and I have a small smile. I'm sitting on my couch.

Also thrilled

Ha!!!!

I am tho

I'm doing work I love today and feeling mellow

Good vibes

Yep!! I hope you're good too

I'm Gucci

Wed 06 Sep

8:05 pm

Hey

Hey I'm at Fairlawn High open house RN

Ok chat later

Yes

Shhhhhhhh

9:45 pm

Hi sweetie
I went out for a glass of wine with my friend after open house

Take me already
Have your way

I know I cannot wait to see you on Saturday
Let's make our plan. Where are we going to meet?

> Any ideas?

> I'd love to sit and have a glass of wine with you somewhere out-of-the-way with tall booths
>
> And then, if you play your cards right, we can go back to your place

> Oh does baby girl think it's gonna be that easy?

> Oh yeah
>
> I can't wait to just hang at your house for hours. I hope that was Ok for me to say. You are the biggest sweetheart and I can't wait to show you how grateful I am for your friendship. Fairlawn plays Highland Square at the football game Friday night

> Oh you can show me whatever you want. We don't have to do anything but kiss and I'd be ok with fulfilling your fantasy. I'll take you wherever you want to go with touch and sexually!

> I don't want to do anything you're not comfortable with

> Thank you I really appreciate that because I think you are way more comfortable with things that I'm not comfortable with yet

> TBH in bed I'm just as nervous but what I want is to just feel free with you and we have shared so many things that we may or may not want to really do. I am open minded and just want to satisfy you

You are so awesome I'm so glad I met you

You say almost everything right and it's been so fun hanging out with you over text

> It's a weird bond, right?

So weird and amazing I don't know about you, but this has never happened to me before

> Me either. It's like I can talk to you without you being offended or so taken back by my fantasy of just wanting to take care of you

The bond is real and it's so fun and awesome

> I try to be respectful of your conservativeness but want you to just explore and have fun. Nothing too crazy just let loose

Thank you so much Babe

> I'll let you thank me soon

> What if you don't like me in person though?

I don't think that's going to change. We have shared things from I would say our minds and soul. My heart is not attached although I Luv this it's more of a fantasy right

> Just FYI, I'm about to pick up my son from Arby's.

Ok chat later baby girl

> Ok but let's start making plans for Saturday. It's coming up very soon

Ok

> Luv u

Luv you too baby girl

>

You better send me a good night pic

> Ok I'll try very hard

No excuses

> But please think of a place we can meet that's not too far away, but still out of the way with tall booths where we can have one glass of wine or one beer

What if you want two glasses of wine?

> I might want two, but that would be the most

I won't take too much advantage of you

I know your limits and rules

>
> I just can't wait to kiss you

If you're lucky

>
> My son is getting in the car now

K

10:58 pm

> Let's make our plan soon

I'm trying to think. I mean what time are you thinking? I think most places will be busy and I'm trying to research and find tall booths for you baby girl to set the mood

>

Yeah that's right

>

What kind of wine do you like?

> Only white. Pinot Grigio, Pinot Noir, Chardonnay. Or beer

Sweeter?

> Less sweet
>
> More dry

Dry like our sex life

Until Saturday

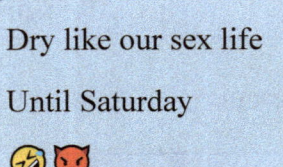

That was a good one eh?

Write that shit down

In Sharpie

Ok sir

Got it

Oh baby yes ma'am

> Are you sure you're ready for this?
>
> We don't have to

> I am!!
>
> I want to
>
> I need to at least kiss you like mad

> I don't want you to feel obligated

> I don't.
>
> Do you have protection in case we go that far?

> Yes ma'am

> And I am clean BTW. I know I talk a good game but I don't sleep around. I like the via text flirting enough not to have to feel the need to bang everything

> Oh that's nice to know. I'm clean too

Oh Babe I know you are

>

Maybe I can make you a little dirty Saturday?

Just a little

>
>
> What time? Where?

You're on a need to know basis

> I can't wait to give you a big hug
>
> And a kiss if you're lucky

I want to play with you under the table, footsie, teasing, touching

With permission

Totally discreet

> Ok. I don't think we're going to last long

You're making me hard now

Who's gonna cave first?

You! 😉

Seriously probably me

How will we know who caves first?

I got an idea

The one who leads the other out the door to our cars is the one who caves first

Nope

Whoever orders the check first. (I'll pay no matter what) but whoever orders the check sends the signal they are ready to have fun

Oh good one

Yes

> I'm telling you I could write porn

Yes you could

> Or some sensual shit

Yep

> Hook a brother up with a contract

I don't know how. If I ever can I will

> I should be charging you FR
>

Yep

> I'm the one being taken advantage of
>
> You like it

> Ooooohhh you are?

We don't have to have sex but can I eat your pussy?

> Yes!!!
>
> You make me laugh

Luv it

I'm pretty funny

> You are Babe
>
> I wouldn't still be around if you didn't make me laugh

Do you have a nice skirt picked out?

> Yes I do
>
> I'm going to look so cute for you

I make you cum that's why you're still around

>

 Well

You are hot as hell

Have fun with me Babe

I am and will

I want to see a look in your eye

Yes

I'm moving to my bedroom now

Can I cum with you?

 see what I did

I do see

Fairlawn plays Highland Square Friday night

Already said this

For real?

Adorable you are

Forgetful I am

If our kids wouldn't be there I would make love to you under the bleachers

Yes!!!

You make me lol

It's so much better being on the phone with you than doom scrolling

Night night Babe

Sweet dreams

You too!!

Thur 07 Sep

8:50 am

Have a great day

You too

Thur 07 Sep

7:42 pm

Hi

Hi

WYD

> Driving

You Alone?

> In a few minutes

Shhhhhh

> You're so cute
> I'm alone now

Let me play with you while you drive

> Ok

I mean my fingers baby girl

> Mmmmm

Keep your eyes on the road

Let me work my magic

> It's not easy, but I am

2 and 10 keep those hands

Seatbelt on right?

> Always

Safety for my baby girl is number one

> I want to sit with you at a bar and have a glass of wine so bad
>
> But I want to sit on the same side of the table

Are you sure you're ready?

> I was ready a while ago, but it just didn't work out
>
> So I am more than ready now

Can we play footsies?

> Yes, sir

Can I brush up against your leg with mine?

> Yes!
>
> Where will we go?

Is it killing you?
Lol

> Yes, it is
>
> Where should we meet?
>
> Where where where?

Are you a planner?

> Kind of yes, but I also love last minute things

I'm a planner but may be it should be a secret

Almost like the scenario mentioned before as if we don't even know if we will go home together

> Yes, I love that
>
> Oh my problem is I don't exactly know what time I'll be free
>
> I just have to make sure my boys are wherever they want to go and then I'll be free unless they're staying home and I can just leave

Do you have an idea?

> I could just tell them that I'm busy at a certain time so maybe we could meet at 7 o'clock? And I can just tell them I have plans and then if they need me before 7 o'clock to drive them somewhere

Low pressure from my end

Whatever is best for you and the boys

Do you watch football?

> Not unless I am snuggled next to a cute guy who wants to watch football

I was going to bet on the Browns game tonight

I don't really pay too much attention to football

> I can bet on the Browns I'll bet that they're going to lose.

If they win what do I get?

If they lose what do you get?

> Oh my goodness I don't know what to say

I think you have an idea

> I don't. I don't know what to say

What do you really want / crave / desire from me?

> That's a juicy awesome question that I have to think about for a minute
>
> You've already given me so much

Games about to start so don't drag your naughty thoughts too long

> I'm not having any naughty thoughts right now that I can think of
>
> I just wanna see you and hang out with you and have a glass of wine and smooch you

Thur 07 Sep

10:30 pm

Hi

Hi Babe. I'm about to fall asleep. Talk tomorrow for sure?

Wet dreams of me please

I beg of you

Fri 08 Sep

7:26 am

12:00 pm

Where's my boo?

Halloween

Yay you're alive!

I was afraid you were ghosting me

> Why?

Because I'm insecure and an emotional wreck

> About what?
>
> Tomorrow?

No not tomorrow. I'm just being silly and because I sent you a heart earlier and didn't hear back for a while. It's just because I'm sitting on my couch writing a lot today, so I keep checking my phone

> Oh
>
> So maybe I haven't said anything but I don't like to be texted until after 8:00 sounds stupid and I'm not trying to be a dick. I'm a light sleeper and my best sleep is from 4:00 to 7:30ish. I sleep with an app on – noise canceling

Oh I see. Thanks for telling me.

> And I'm going to a concert tonight so if I'm not as playful it's because I'm busy

> Ok. Have fun!

Sat 09 Sep

> 12:24 am

> I hope your concert was amazing

< It was mind blowing
< I'm so into them now

> Who did you see?

< Greta Van Fleet
< Heard of 'em?

> Definitely heard of them but I'm looking them up on YouTube right now

< I'm going to marry the singer

> The guy?

> YES ma'am
>
> Listen to his voice
>
> Mmmmmmmmm

> Oh my god you're so hot right now
>
> He does sound amazing
>
> Who do they remind me of? I can't think of it

> Led Zeppelin

> Yes
>
> Bingo
>
> They sound freaking awesome

> The singer has stage presence like Prince

> Oh my god, I love that
>
> You're so lucky you got to see them

> I got chills a couple times

> That is incredible. I'm so happy for you
>
> I can't wait to see you

I'm nervous

> Awwww me too but it'll be amazing
>
> You still want to right, tell me the truth
>
> Or do you want to just keep up our fantasy texting life

I'm torn. It's so hot what we have done

I'm leaning more to yes I'm just nervous

I want to live up to the hype 😉

> I totally hear ya. Yeah, there's been a lot of hype. But you could say it's not really hype. It's really us talking to each other over text.
>
> I'm not sure what we should do but I would love to meet you
>
> But I'd rather play it the way you want to play it

Nic sends me a song through Spotify: You're The Only One by Greta Van Fleet.

> Listen to this one

Ok I'll listen right now

Awww I love that

Have a good night Babe. Talk tomorrow

> Sweet dreams
>
> You in bed?

I'm on the couch still but I'm half asleep. I had two beers.

> Naughty girl

I know, but my friend Julie drove me so it was fine

> Is Julie single?

> She is actually
>
> She may be my only single friend

Hook a brother up

> No way you're mine

Feisty baby girl

> Do you know you can have me as soon as you say the word?

Nope. I want you to say it

> You can have me you're just not sure you want me IRL

Wait what?

No I want you to tell me to take you (have you). Like submit to me

I am horrible at first moves

> You already made like moves one through 10 so you don't have to worry about that
>
> You've done more than enough foreplay over the last month or two

It's different in person

> I know it's different in person, but we still have this history

Yes I don't discredit the history. I'm just a shy guy naturally with women

I could never ask a woman out at the gym or a bar

No BALLS

Lol

> You don't seem like that over text
>
> You seem to know exactly what you want

I know and that's why I like it because I'm good at it this way

> You are super good at it this way

> Should we just go get a drink somewhere and then decide then if we want to do anything more?
>
> You'll never upset me. I'll never be offended by you
>
> Do you want me to kiss you first?

You can do whatever you want

I am yours

> Then, why don't we just meet and see how we feel?
>
> And if I feel like kissing you, I will and if you feel like kissing me, you should

I'm trying not to be naughty right now

My cock is throbbing

I wish you could feel it right now pulsating in you

> I wish I could too
>
> I feel it in my imagination
>
> I do get the sense that you don't really want to meet in person and I want you to know I'm fine either way

No that's not true

The only sense is I'm nervous as if I was meeting anyone new

Just anxious

> Is there any way we could make it less anxious for you?

It's like this. I've said some things to you that's inappropriate and I'm kinda shy about meeting face to face saying those things

> I totally understand but somehow I'm not as nervous as you are

Like if we are having sex I would never tell you to put my cock in your mouth. But I'll type that shit 🤷

> I actually love that

Wait which part?

> I think in person I am more traditional than what we've done over text
>
> So if you're less kinky in person, I would actually like that

I will treat you like a virgin

I like hot steamy sex. No whips and chains

> I like that
>
> I just wish we could not put any pressure on ourselves
>
> And just meet
>
> With no other expectations

We both want to be intimate with each other

> Yes
>
> But no strings attached and no promises for the future
>
> Doesn't that sound good?

Yes baby girl exactly

>

Fulfilling fantasy Safe Fun

> So what if we just met out for a glass of wine or a beer and then decided if we wanted to go to your place?

> We are coming back to my place silly. Yes a drink for sure before so I can relax 🤭❤️

Ok good

I know it'll be weird at first but I'm sure after five minutes we'll be fine

> Same side of the table 🥺😉

Good memory yes that would be fine but I'd also like to sit on the opposite side

> The urge to make you wet is overwhelming
> 😉
> No footsies

You've been making me wet for like two months 😆

I think we've both waited long enough

> Babe you've been busy. I've been doing laps at Edgewater waiting for you
> Lol

>
> Yes I've had periods of being super busy since I met you and also super sad. I'm sorry about that.

No apology. I'm messing

If you're sorry you can show me how sorry you are tomorrow

>
> But I'm going to have to ask you why you want me to set you up with Julie? 😅

It was exactly to get you to say what you did

You claimed me

> Ha!!! Yes

The feeling of being claimed ya know?

> It worked

Maybe I'll show you how it feels to be consumed tomorrow and kinda owned

I could not tell you that on the phone but I'll type it

Lol

You're my birthday partner

Bring your birthday suit and we will talk

Ha!!!!

I'll be wearing it

Not for long

You will probably order the check when she sets the drinks down to be served

> Hopefully we can get through one drink

And I will follow orders after that

> That's right

Yes dear

>

How many times do you think I can make you cum tomorrow?

> Oh my gosh I have no idea

I like goals

Make it realistic for you

> Then I'll say one
>
> I think the female orgasm is pretty mysterious

> Is it tough for you normally?

Kind of yes

> Ok, no worries
> Just relax with me

Sometimes it's easier when I'm by myself
I will relax

> Your hips too
> And that muscle

Ok.

> Pretty sure I can take you there
> Are you ready

I'm ready to meet my Daddy

> Do you have a time frame yet? No biggie if not

> I think whatever we want we should do and I'll tell the boys my plans and if they need me or my car it'll be before that
>
> Want to say eight or nine?

8:00 sounds good but flexible. Let's explore each other. Even if you don't want to have sex we can make out and foreplay

Pretty sure that's the the recipe for hot sloppy sex too tho

> ok
>
> Sounds good
>
> Sounds perfect
>
> You always know what to say to me

I'm game for whatever and how far you want to go

> I love that
>
> Thank you

I'll feed off of you and won't go too far

> Ok 🥲
>
> Ty so much

You can tomorrow

So we can't have kids right?
Sorry covering ground rules and boundaries

We absolutely cannot have kids

You like french kiss?

Love it

Can I pull your hair gently but firmly?

I've never done that, so I don't know

Noted
Do you like to give oral?

> I kind of do, but I'm worried that we haven't shown each other STD test results
>
> I think my kids are about to come home

Oh geez well I'm not that much of a whore. I understand your concern. But I'm clean.

> I don't think you're a whore, but it just takes one to get a disease
>
> I'm getting tested in about one week but I know I'm clean

Well I donated plasma a couple weeks ago and they tell you the results if they are positive for anything

> Ok. Oh my gosh a few weeks ago I was thinking of doing that. I'm not even joking.
>
> Is it super hard? Have you done it more than once?

It's a funny story and I want to tell it to you in person. It's a layered and long one. So good for tomorrow while we have that drink

> Ok cool. I'm excited to hear it
>
> I can't believe how in line we are on some things because it was literally probably two weeks ago that I was looking into donating plasma

> Do you need a safe word for tomorrow?

Probably

> I don't think I'll cross a line but I don't want to overestimate your needs and wants. Also if you use the word it's a STOP and I won't be able to restart because a NO is a NO to me.
> Make sense?

Kind of. Can it just be stop that one thing and not stop entirely?

> Yes
>
> I think I'll be able to tell just by me paying attention to you
>
> I'm just wanting you to feel safe

Thank you very much

I can imagine maybe needing to say be more gentle at times

> Maybe I need a safe word

> Maybe

I'm not really even rough.

I just want to be super gentle and intentional with you

> Awwwwww
>
> I just want to be super close to you naked

Oh that's it?

> 😁😂

I'll make you eat your words baby girl

> I guess while we're texting it's pretty impossible not to tease each other

You like it and you know what you're doing

Who won the football game?

Fairlawn?

> Yes
>
> It was an amazing game actually
>
> Baby girl is tired

Lay your head on my chest and fall asleep

> Ooooohhhhhh my god I want that so badly right now

Stay hydrated you're gonna need it

> How come

Cum honey

> I don't get it

I'm going to make you cum so much you will be dehydrated

> Oh my goodness
>
> Wow

Yeah I said it

Well typed it

> I'm thirsty right now so I better get water before I go to bed

Sweet dreams

> It's been so fun to be so vulnerable with you over text all these weeks
>
> I'm glad to know I'm not the only one who stepped out of her comfort zone and that you did too

Let's agree to be that vulnerable in person too then

> Ok but that might be hard for me at first

Yup me too

> You seem so entirely not shy that that's hard to believe but I do believe you
>
> I'm just saying you come across as not shy for the most part

I wish I was this confident

> But you certainly are this confident in this context

It's like my brain is split gentleman and kink

> Yes it is

I want to excel at both

Best of both worlds

How are you not wet right now?

> I am wet right now

I know

And for me, you've succeeded at the gentleman side and the kinky side

I know what my baby girl likes

You do 💯

I've been paying attention

You have

Like a good boy

You definitely have

I think you've been taking notes

I'm sorry I should leave you be now

> Well, I'm loving chatting with you but I should probably just go to sleep now. I have to take Daniel to Cleveland at 10:30 in the morning.

Understand completely Ok Babe sweet dreams and if I'm in your dreams please just fuck my brains out

I know it's not your style. But try it

> I will gladly try it
>
>
>
> Nighty night

Chapter 12
Last Minute Cancellation

Sat 09 Sep

4:42 pm

I have a sore throat today

Is that your excuse

I still really want to meet up with you, but I'm not completely myself and I don't want to get you sick if you're concerned about that. I'm really sad about it

You are so cute.

I'm nervous but I want to touch you and smell you and see you but I'm nervous

Oh I mean I have a sore throat too

> What should we do? I have every intention of meeting you but I wanted to be at my best
>
> And if you're nervous, I don't want to push you. I'm truly not nervous I just don't feel well
>
> I mean a little bit nervous but nothing too much

How can you not be?

> I am a little bit but I'm still so looking forward to it

I have anxiety when meeting new people. It's nothing you did or said it's just me

> Oh I see
>
> It feels like we already know each other though

I don't do this stuff. I know I say a lot of stuff and you think I'm a confident male but I am further from it

I agree we do have a bond and I do know you. It's just that initial face to face embarrassment

> I know

> Then I said why would I pass up the opportunity to meet you and have us fulfill a fantasy? Nothing hardcore we don't even have to have sex just touch would be amazing and if we have sex then that's fine too. Why would a guy pass that up 🤍🔥🤍
>
> I'm just sharing with you how human I am and not just a horny guy. I mean I'm always horny but I have a heart too
>
> It's like I feel guilty at the same time. I feel maybe I've made you do and say things that are not true to you so I feel like a sleeze ball
>
> Does this all make sense what I'm typing?

> It makes total sense, and you are a sweetheart
>
> But everything I did I wanted to do and when I didn't want to do anything any longer I let you know
>
> It has been so fun chatting with you all these weeks
>
> Sometimes for me, it's better to do something on short notice rather than planning it way ahead
>
> Because I feel terrible that we planned this so far ahead and now I don't feel well

I'm not worried about your sore throat. Sounds like you just need something to coat the back of it 👀

Do you want to just not see each other tonight but then sometime just see if we want to see each other on very short notice?

The problem is I also have a headache that I can't kick. That's the main reason I don't feel well. Plus the sore throat is something you could catch but I hear you that you don't care about that

Please

All jokes aside

I'm down for tonight

Yes I'm nervous but I set aside the night for you.

If you don't feel well enough to have fun I understand and I won't be the least bit mad

I'm fine with whatever you decide. I know headaches can be shitty.
Please low pressure just let me know

> You are the best
>
> I was really looking forward to tonight and I had a sore throat for a few days and I was going to ignore it but my headache today is hard to ignore. Do you like my idea of not planning way ahead and just seeing when the next time we can both meet up will be?
>
> I want to give you my all, and I don't feel like I have much to give today

What if I just take what you have to offer?

I'll flirt you back into coming out tonight so you don't give me that option 🤣

> We could do that.
> I just wanted the first time you met me to be at my best, but maybe I shouldn't care about that

> I have no expectations on who or what you are
>
> I won't know a best from a worst
>
> What if I make your headache go away?

I'm not sure what the best thing to do is.

That's a possibility that I like the sound of

I don't think I'll be drinking any alcohol tonight though. I wouldn't mind a Shirley Temple though

> Lame

I know right?

> It would probably make your headache go away but I'll take the credit

I'm starting to feel a little better. Just texting with you.

One thing that often helps my headaches is a back rub

Like on the neck and shoulders

> We can skip the bar and I can just give you a rub down

< That's very tempting tonight

> What kind of wine do you like?

< Any dry white
< Red gives me headaches

> We don't want that

< Yep
< Do you have a couch?

> Yes but your too lanky for it lol It's a two seater

< What does lanky mean?

> TALL
>

> Ooohhh ha
>
> Maybe we can just cuddle on your couch and I can get a back rub

And shoulder

> Yes

I have a king size bed that fits you lanky chicks better

Lol

> Hee hee

I'm down for whatever. I want you comfortable

How tall are you again?

> 5 feet 5 inches

> Oh I thought you were taller in my head
>
> All the pics you send you seem tall

It's probably the angle I take the pictures

I just wanna curl up on a couch tonight

Is it OK if I think about it a little bit longer?

> Yes think away Babe

Thank you 🥲

> I can give you a few things to think about lol

😅

Are you ever down for getting together at the last minute?

> Yes
>
> Stakes might be a little different
>
> Role play may be a little different
>
> Vibe may be a little different

> I kind of understand what you're saying but not totally

It is all meant to be playful

> Oh ok I got you then

I send Nic a pic of my left hand with my fingers curled down onto my palm showing my blue polished nails.

> I got my nails done for you and everything

Don't be getting me all worked up

>
>
> I just want you to know this is terrible timing and I don't want it to be this way.
>
> I didn't want to be sick today but I caught what Daniel has
>
> He got a bad cold after the jazz festival

> No worries Babe. Do NOT feel guilty at all

Thank you and I didn't want to tell you yesterday because I was hoping I'd be better today but I hate messing with your plans

> With me always tell me as soon as a shift in plans happens. I can respond better to that as I can then shift and plan something else.
>
> I'm the same way at work. Call in as early as possible so I can help get the shift covered.

I hear ya

> We can just communicate another time. It might be a shorter time and we have to skip the bar and meet at my place.

Yes

So let's skip tonight and I'm heartbroken over it

I really truly don't mean to keep canceling on you

This is why short notice is sometimes better for me

No need for an apology I'll let you make it up to me 🔥👀😈

Ok I will

Be careful what you agree to 😉👀

🤣

Sat 09 Sep

9:12 pm

Hey

WYD

Lying in bed in the dark, half asleep with my kitty watching TV

Not even a good night pic? 🤣

> I feel so sick Babe

Drink some OJ

Or whiskey

> I have neither of those but I do have vodka and lemonade

Get some rest Babe

> Ok thank you
>
> Thank you for checking on me

Sun 10 Sep

12:12 pm

> How ya feeling?

> I am a lot better today but still not 100% but much better. Thank you for checking on me. I'm an hour away with Daniel at a rehearsal.

> Oh. Ok chat later.

> Ok I'm by myself for now. I'm heading to Panera to do work on my computer

> I'm walking into the gym

> Oh nice be sure to pump up those muscles for me 😁

Sun 10 Sep

2:16 pm

> I can hang out today between five and nine approximately if you'd like

Sun 10 Sep

10:21 pm

You in bed?

No

You?

Eating a snack

Did you get my text that I was able to see you tonight?

Yes

No pressure. Just wondering.

You ever wake up from a deep nap and you can't get any energy going?

Yes

> How was the rehearsal?

It was good. I got a project done and it was beautiful weather today. How was your day?

> Worked out did laundry and chores and relaxed

Nice

I'm ready to live my life more fully. I'm handling missing Will a bit better now. I'm excited to meet you in person but it's totally fine if you don't want that. I just want you to know that I'm ready to 'date' out in the real world. Not looking to be exclusive. So let me know if you ever want to meet for a drink and a little footsie

> I want to play footsie

Ok cool

Next chance we get we'll meet up

> It's gonna be hot and steamy
>
> I promise

> I know it will be. I really can't wait.

Sun 10 Sep

8:21 pm

> Hi

Hi?

> It's Natalie
> Use this number from now on.
> Please delete the other number

Natalie who?

> It's my Google voice number

Natalie who?

> Natalie. Your not girlfriend girlfriend

> Tell me something only you would know 😉

Ummmm.

We both like to play footsie

And I know you have boy girl twins and I know when your birthday is

> Is this a new you new vibe and attitude? You are never aggressive
>
> Lol
>
> Sure you want me to delete or just not use that number?
>
> Can you send conservative pics on this phone at least?

I guess just don't use that other number

This is more private

No racy pics still. Sorry.

> No need for apology
>
> I'm always gonna try
>
> I am a guy
>
> And you're so fucking cute

> Awwwww
>
>
>
> I want you to see me in my cute little dress looking cute for you soon

Baby girl I want that too

Be ready this week

> I wasn't able to meet yesterday and you weren't today 😢
>
> I'll be ready this week

I'm hunting you

> Should we just have a drink at your place or should we meet out? I can't decide

I want you to be comfortable with whatever we do.

> Mmmmm

> We are still strangers and I respect a woman's concerns for privacy
>
> If it's gonna be a quick meeting probably my place. If it's a timed meeting we can meet at a bar first.
> I'm comfortable with both and nervous for both
>
> I'm human

>> That's all good

> I'm very feisty RN

>> I was earlier. I was ready to hop in my car and go to you
>>
>> We're only partially strangers in my opinion

> So I can do to you things strangers can't?

>> That's a good question
>>
>> I would say yea
>>
>> I feel like I know you

> Precisely maybe why I made you wait
>
> We know each other better than most spouses

> Yes!!!

Not girlfriend girlfriend

> We're here for each other

Absolutely

> Don't you love that? NOT GF GF

Sounds hot

> It is hot right?

> I feel like I can read your moods

I doubt you can read that dark

> I can read dark I think

I want to take over your body and make you cum more than you ever have

> You melt me
>
> I have to be with you soon

I would make love to you on your balcony if you could be quiet enough

> Omg

Could you?

> You're killing me
>
> That is an amazing picture in my mind

Can you be discreet on a nature trail?

> No I can't
>
> I wish I could

> Could you wear a dress and let me enter you on a nature trail and if we heard someone coming be able to hide it?
>
> Or are you loud?

I need to get off the phone now

> Yes ma'am

TEN MINUTES PASS BY

We could try that

My son needed my phone for a second

I would like to try that but I'm afraid of bugs and getting caught

> Are we safe?
>
> Bugs that's the hot part
>
>

Yes we're safe now

Bugs love me

I hate them

> I want to taste you

>> Mmmmm
>> I want you to kiss me

> Soft on the lips and neck

>> Please please
>> I can't wait

> I want you so bad

>> Same
>> I really can't wait
>> When did we meet

> Never

>> Oh. Oops.

> Wrong boy toy

No!!!

What do you call the day we both learned each other existed then?

> Start date of your wildest fantasy

When did we virtually meet then?

> Like 2019 FR

Ha! Why do you say that?

> It feels like forever

And yes, you are my wildest fantasy

I'll be right back I have to go brush my teeth

> K

>> I'm back
>>
>> It does feel like forever
>>
>> You helped me through some serious shit

> That's what I'm here for

>> I feel like we get along really well
>>
>> Even though you say we've never met
>>
>> I think we've met, just not face-to-face
>>
>> You know what I mean

> There is still an element of shock in the process

>> Yes
>>
>> I know
>>
>> I just want to get the first time over with so then we can just hang out whenever we want on short notice
>>
>> I just want to look extra cute and be in my cute dress the first time and not having a raging headache

> Oh baby girl
>
> All for me?

Yes!!!!!!!

I love music and love that you sent me that song the other night

> Do you know the things I want to do with you?

I don't know, can you tell me?

Send me songs you love any time you want

> My music is very different than you like

I liked the Greta Van Fleet song

> Which one?

I remember one of the first hot things I wrote you

> What did you write?

> I wrote that I wanted you to put your hand down my panties

Do I still have permission?

> Yes please do
>
> I need you to
>
> If we meet at a bar for a glass of wine, I might just be giggling the entire time

My fingers are magical

> Hhhmmmmm show me

If we meet at a bar?
Pretty sure that's a given

> I'm very wet

Don't stop
Let's cum

> I want more than your fingers

I'll give you both if you are a good girl
Can you feel me?

> Yes

Relax the hips and push those toes to the sky

> My pussy wants you

I want your mind to want me

> Come in

I want your soul to want me too

> Yes, we need to meet Tim
>
> Meet very soon
>
> Not Tim
>
> It's hard to text with one hand

Keep the other hand busy Babe, no worries

> Ok
>
> Where r u?
>
> You get me so hot

I would make you squirt right now if we were together

> I want you

Have me

> Ok
>
> Can you meet tomorrow night? Where are you?

I'm home 😉

> I need you now
>
> In my bed

Cum with me

> Last night my son slept in my room.
>
> I have two twin beds in my room. If he ever comes in unexpectedly I'll just have to stop texting

Ok. no worries

> I want to
>
> So bad
>
> I want to go out with you tomorrow night
>
> Night night Babe

Let me lick you up and down

> Please please do

> Even your private spot

> I'm half asleep. Thanks for tonight's fun

> Let me see you

Nic sends me a selfie of his face and bare chest.

> Awwwww
>
> You look so good
>
> I can't take a pic in the dark

> Flash silly

Mon 11 Sep

8:38 am

I send Nic a song from Spotify:

Fleetwood Mac - Hold Me

A song for you

I send Nic a selfie. I'm wearing my favorite rust colored tee shirt and my hair is pulled back in a pony tail. I'm wearing gold earrings, a smirky smile and white jeans that show just a little in the corner of the pic.

Mon 11 Sep

6:52 pm

Hi ya

Let me have you

I want to

Come here

Omg. Hold on.

I will but I need a little time. Can I come in like an hour?

Are you sure you are ready?

> I'm not sure but I'm coming anyway. I've been thinking about you all day. I'm not in my cute little dress though

I was kinda kidding about tonight. I was talking shit

But I'll go with the flow

> You are freaking me out

Why?

> Never mind.

I'm trying to drive you nuts

I don't care what you wear it will be bedside anyways 😊

Are you serious about coming?

> I was

Ok

'I am' sounds better tho

But you are the writer

> I was. I'm not now.

Why what's up?
I hope I didn't scare you

I'm a little confused and would like clarification

> I'm freaked out that you said: I was kinda kidding about tonight. I was talking shit.

So I was just throwing flirts in the air. I didn't think you would say yes. It was very last minute and made me nervous.

Just like OMG this is happening nervous

> I know. I get it. I'm not coming tonight but like I said yesterday you can practically say the word and I'll come over but tonight I got the wind knocked out of my sails. I'm not as nervous as you and I totally respect that but because of that I'm going to be very careful about making sure you want me to come over

Well no silly I was just like I said flirting. I want you to come over. I was just surprised you were available at a moments notice

> Well, I'm sorry I took it very seriously

Yuck to texting

Sorry I knocked the wind out. I didn't mean to if anything I was trying to drive you nuts and want me more

If you hurry you'll still catch me air drying from my shower

So no for tonight?

> I'm sorry I can't. This is a pretty big deal so next time when it comes up don't mess around about it please then I'll feel better about coming over.
> Also the ball is in your court.

> I guess you didn't mean to but you stunned me. I'm sorry.

You stunned me Babe with agreeing to come over. No way was I expecting it.

Well I want you tonight. But I'm not gonna be forceful about it. Sorry for the miscommunication.

> Ok. I'm sorry. I did ask you about tonight last night and i also said that I'm often better with last minute plans better than planning ahead

> Because my life can be unpredictable with the boys

And that's why I was stunned I was expecting you to be obligated to the boys with a school function or whatever

Now I feel like I'm begging you to come over

> I don't think you're begging at all.

Ok

> I'm sorry. I still want to but not tonight

Ok I get it just know my schedule is tight this week. We can try again soon tho.

> Ok

> Yes
>
> I'm sorry Nic. I was waiting for you to ask me to come over and then you did and then you took it back. I'm sorry I'm being so emotional about this. Please let me know when you want to see me even if it's last minute. I'm sometimes free at the last minute. Or it can be planned ahead ♥ ♥

K

>

I want to taste you

> You sent a shiver right down through me

< I want to cuddle you so tight

> I want you to

< I've never done stuff like this. It's deep so I'm a little guarded and you're super guarded and now open like a flood gate. I want you and I wish it could have been tonight but maybe it's best because you wouldn't have been able to handle it.

> I want to handle it. I was ready for you tonight.
>
> You are more scared than I am, mister.
>
> I want to hug you and kiss you

< It's not scared. I feel guilty for changing you from day one. You were so innocent and never had a thought like this in your mind and then I come along and turn you naughty

> I love that you feel responsible. You did bring something out of me. But don't feel guilty. It's been amazing. You have lightened my life. You are exactly what I needed

Touch me

> Pretend or IRL

Don't even with me lady. You turned me down once today

Kidding relax just getting you hyped up

> I kind of want to come now. What do you think?

Babe I'm a little vulnerable now

> What do you mean?
>
> Another night. I hope soon

A few drinks and super sensual and a hint of horny

I'd rather start off together with a drink. You are right. You had a head start.

I could show you but I learned my lesson before

You're not ready for this Babe

Thank you for being a gentleman

Please let me come over one of these days

I'm going to rock your world I just want to make sure you are ready

I'm ready but you'll be gentle right? And conservative the first time?

Yes Babe I know I talk shit and dark stuff. I'm more into touch and foreplay and hot steamy basic sex

Ok I like that

> I can't even envision rough sex with you
>
> It's not our energy
>
> And not my vibe
>
> Understood?

Thank you Babe

> Oh you will. Trust me
>
> Same moment you regret not coming over tonight!
>
>

Hee hee 😄

> I have a naughty request

You can try me

> At least for the first time we make love I want you to look into my eyes when you cum. I want to see you enjoy it

> Ok but my eyes are often closed

You've never really felt it then that's ok. I'll show you what it feels like

> I have felt it but I close my eyes usually I think

Not when I want you to look into my eyes watch me watch you feel it and see it in my eyes

Your pleasure is my pleasure

> That sounds amazing. I maybe too shy though

I don't think you have a choice

And I don't think you're gonna wanna keep your eyes off of me 😉

> I'm melting
>
> You have a way with words.
> So have we all but decided we're skipping the whole glass of wine at a bar idea?

> No way that would be so fucking hot. All the young servers watching us flirt and just be so immature and drool over the menu over each other
>
> Discreet high top is a priority
>
> Me touching you inappropriately in my bed is mandatory ♥

Yes to ALL THAT

Where will we go? We need a tall booth.

> I've got a few places picked out if this is the scenario

Ok. Great.

Thank you for doing that homework. You get an A plus.

> Excuse me I am the teacher
>
> I do the grading

You are the principal actually

> Then why are you talking back?

> Seems like we have our own private office

Yes we do

You like that don't you?

> YES YES

I'm so naughty RN

> Yes you are

Let me clear my desk off by swiping my arm over it so you can sit on it

> So you can lay me across it?

> Are you gonna ride me on my own desk?

< Yes!!!!

> You can't have any clothes on

< Ok sir

> Relax your hips

< Ok

> You're in control relax the hips so it goes in deeper

< Mmmmmmm

> That's a good girl
>
> Just like that
>
> Ma'am

> Let me know when you look at me

Night night. Tomorrow is my first day teaching in 2 years

> I'm going to take advantage of you one day. I want you so bad. With permission of course

Please please I can't wait for you

> What do you crave right now?

Besides you? Sleep.

> Let me make you cum then you can sleep

Ok hold on

> I already put it all the way in so there is no holding on

I have to

Hold on

I'm crawling into bed with you now

> I just want you

I love when you say that

It's my favorite

> Let me see you

I don't take nighttime in the dark pictures. I'm sorry. They're always horrible

That's why I give you daytime pretty pictures

That wasn't my asking voice

Oh my

Understood?

That gave me tingles
I want to hang out with you

Prove it

How?

Oh that's right it's too dark

Yes

> You may not be able to walk to your car after I have my way with you based on your words

> > You may have to carry me
> >
> > I'm busy from Tuesday through Friday night this week
> >
> >

> Hence why tonight was critical

> > Because of our schedules?

> I knew tonight was my only opening for the week that's why I spoke up

> > I'm sorry I got so freaked out by that one text that I couldn't hide it or pretend I didn't

> I just want to touch you

> > I want you to so badly
> >
> > Are you free Saturday night?

> I have the kids

Oh ok.

Sunday night?

> Have the kids till evening

Starting Sunday and next week the only thing that could interfere is my time of the month starts I'm out of commission for a solid week usually 😢😢

> Tomorrow?

Have to take Daniel to a rehearsal in Cleveland and we get back at 10

Do you have any days off this week that you would have time during?

One of these days they'll be buying a car and I'll have a lot more freedom

> What about Wednesday?

> Wednesday day or night?

It's ok

#busyhotmomlife

> Actually it doesn't matter I have no time Wednesday
>
> You make me laugh so hard

That's my one day off

> How can you be so cute?
>

Don't ever turn me down again. I want you too bad

> I won't. I swear.

Just take it from now on

> But then, no sarcasm about me coming over because you can't read sarcasm over text

Don't talk back little girl you should have known better

> Take what?
>

My flirts

My fantasy wishes

>
> I want you

You should have cum here

> I should have, but I got super freaked out.

I wasn't expecting to see you today. I'm sorry.

> I wonder if we'll have to just meet at 11 o'clock one night

You would be in bed and too tired

Probably true

We know each other so well, it's so weird

So not even Sunday night after your kids leave if I'm not having my monthly bill?

Tues 12 Sep

11:48 am

I'm sorry we didn't end last night like we wanted to. I fell asleep.

No worries chic

Tues 12 Sep

3:38 pm

Dare I even ask?

Ask what?

But yes, you should dare ask. Always opt for asking.

Can I make sweet love to you tonight?

The problem is, I won't be back at home until 10 o'clock.

Where ya headed to?

They have a rehearsal at Severance Hall in Cleveland

From 7 to 9

> Yeah I wouldn't ask you to drive all the way home and back down to my place. Just know I want you so bad

> I know and I feel the same

Tues 12 Sep

11:15 pm

> You up?

> Yes but on the phone with Will

> K chat later if you can

11:43 pm

> I just had an amazing phone call with Will

> Awe

He was enthusiastic to talk to me. It was amazing.

> Sounds amazing

It was, thank you. For some reason both of them were happy to talk to me whereas in the past 2 or 3 weeks they've just been kind of pissy

> Who's both?

I mean, I don't care if my ex is happy to talk to me, but it really helps me be able to talk to Will.

How are you?

> Honestly?

Yes

> I'm horny AF

Oooohhhh

> Yeah sorry

We have to figure something out

I'm sorry

Our plans keep getting messed up

> Oh yea like what?
>
> Don't be sorry I'm flirting
>
> I want to figure out how many times I can make you cum in one night

When can we see each other?

> Tell me the earliest you would want to see me.
> Be careful

> Ok let me see
>
> It's not a matter of only availability
>
> I'd say Monday night but it's possible I won't be able to that night bc of my female body so I hate to get our hopes up again and then crash them

Do you like sex in the day time?

> I think I do. I love night though
>
> Bc night we can go get a drink and flirt and then go home to your place
>
> And I can wear something cute to make you swoon

When do you think you start your female situation?

> Somewhere around Sunday could be a day or two before or a day or two after

I'm off tomorrow that's why I ask

> BTW love how you word stuff ♥️
>
> Oh my I can't tomorrow. I'm so bummed.

No worries you're not ready for me anyways

> I so am
>
> Are you sure not Sunday night?

Maybe I'll make you wait til Monday

Or even Tuesday

> Those are iffy days for me

Every day is fucking iffy with you

When do you want to make love damnit?

> Saturday Sunday

> Aren't you bleeding to death then?

Maybe or not until like Tuesday

> Will you be in the mood?

I will if I haven't started bleeding yet

> I mean Tuesday. Isn't that the end you're soooo confusing

> I wish to satisfy your fantasy

My period is supposed to start in the range of Saturday to Tuesday

And then it lasts for six or seven days

> Christ sakes like pulling teeth for the schedule
>
> 7 days fuck sake

> I know. If it's not that long I'll be over
>
> It varies

Gotta wait another week

>

Chapter 13
I Want You NOW

Wed 13 Sep

8:53 am

Morning

Hi

Come here

> Then don't. I want you NOW

I have an appointment from 10 to 11 I think pretty close to your house. Should I come after that?

I have maybe an hour I could meet with you

Cause I can't wait anymore

> I don't want to be pushy

You're not

I have a lot to do today, but I'm right down the road from you and I can't wait anymore

> I won't take anymore time than you give me

Please can I come at that time?

> Are you ready for that?

> I am beyond ready. I've canceled too many times

Will you be wet on arrival?

> 100%

What time?

> 11:10

ABOUT ONE HOUR LATER

9:56 am

> I just drove over a curb. I'm so distracted. I hope I didn't do any damage to my car.
>
> I'm scared that I did… but after this appointment at 11 I'm driving to your apartment
>
> I think my car is fine it just didn't sound good

I'll be patiently waiting

I can't believe it

I want to touch myself or should I save it for you?

You should save it

Ok. You're going to make me cum really quick tho. I won't be down and out but that's your warning

Don't be coming over here shy and shit

Act on your words, feel free and relax with me.

Natalie is at her therapist appointment from 10 to 11 am

11:05 am

I'm getting in the car now

Drive safe

Very funny

> Where are you?

> > I'm five minutes away

> It's confusing when you pull in – head to the back make a right on Tinkerton
>
> Do you want me to come get you from parking lot or you walk up?

> > Please meet me out there somewhere. I always get lost in apartments

11:10 am

> Are you close

> > I think so yes

11:12 am

> > Here

My excitement and anticipation to finally see Nic was building to a crescendo. I couldn't believe we were finally about to meet in person. There had been so many cancellations and delays. So much drama and life getting in the way.

I hadn't been very nervous to meet him leading up to this moment. But this morning, once I realized that our first meeting would actually happen today, the nerves and excitement just about took me over completely.

During my entire therapy appointment that morning, I couldn't hold back a small, smirky smile, knowing I was going to be face to face with Nic in less than an hour. The session with my therapist was really great, despite my internal battle fighting the butterflies dancing around inside me.

As soon as I got to the parking area for Nic's apartment, I slowed down my car. I was looking for him to be there to guide me in, but I didn't see him. Then he suddenly peeked out from between two cars and waved at me with the biggest smile. Without thinking about it, I took my hands off the steering wheel and clapped several times in the air. I was overjoyed to see him. I wasn't even consciously aware that I was clapping. The wait was finally over.

I got out of my car and he came over to me. We walked hand in hand to his door. The excitement was palpable. As we walked the path to his apartment, I was amazed at just how big his chest and arms were in person. I imagined myself sinking into them soon.

We got inside and I tried not to let the nerves overtake me. I took my shoes off. We hugged. A long, tight hug. We did not kiss, though. It was a pure, romantic and loving hug. He said, "We've been through so much together." And it was the perfect thing to say at that moment.

I sat down on his couch and he sat on his chair. But he was much too far away so I said, "Can you sit over here next to me," as I patted the couch to my left. So he got up from his chair and moved over next to me.

I immediately curled up to him, taking his right arm in both my arms and putting my head on his shoulder. He had been such a good friend to me all these weeks. He had been patient and kind and funny and so damn sexy. I just wanted to sit in this moment and seal it into my memory. I'm so glad I did because I can still picture it as if it were yesterday.

After we sat for a while and talked and laughed, I knew I had to finally kiss him. I also knew he was not going to make the first move. He is a true gentleman. So I lifted my chin up to his face and he gently kissed my lips. His lips surrounded by his beard were so soft and inviting. I was melting as I had been for seven weeks. But now, IRL.

I turned my body to face him and we kissed some more. I was so wet from just anticipating seeing him this morning and then from finally seeing him in the parking lot and now, from his sweet, soft lips against mine.

I knew I wanted to be with him today more closely than this so I asked, "Do you want to go lie down in your room?" He said yes in the cutest way. We stood up, he took my hand and led me to his bedroom.

It was midday, so his bedroom was bright. In my married life, I would not have wanted to be intimate in all that light. But with Nic, it didn't matter to me whatsoever. I felt unconditional acceptance from him. The passion I had for him and the craving for his touch were all that mattered.

Nic laid me down on his bed. I noted black sheets, just like I have on my own bed. I felt safe with him and yet ready for anything. The respect and comfort he had been promising me were there in that bedroom 100%. With Nic, I knew I'd be willing to try so many things sexually that I had never dared entertain before. Nic was my guide. My hot, muscular, gentleman guide. The words he wrote to me the first day we ever texted came back to me at that moment, "Put your seatbelt on and enjoy the ride," and I couldn't help but giggle out loud.

Nic playfully tugged at my lips with his teeth while we were kissing. This was new to me. The gentle pull between pain and pleasure was almost too much to bear. His kisses were soft and gentle but magnetic, just like he hinted they would be. He was hard by the time we got to the bedroom and so I let him slip right inside of me because both of us had waited far too long for this.

He surprised me by pulling himself up above me and taking hold of my ankles. He held my legs straight up and out in a huge V. He managed to do this while he was gently pressing himself into me – in and out. This position allowed us to laser focus on finally coming together after so many sexy, hot texts where we could only imagine what this was going to feel like.

He came back down on top of me and I grabbed what I could of his intensely muscular back. I couldn't fully wrap my hands around his arms and that turned me on even more. I lost myself in his driving body. I took my right leg and somehow flung it up above his shoulder. I wanted to envelop him. I couldn't get him close enough. I had not felt this level of heat with a man in a very long time, if ever.

When we were done, we cuddled tightly on his bed. I was laughing. Almost uncontrollably. I kept saying over and over, "That was so fun." I felt giddy like a schoolgirl. My smile was ear to ear. Nic was laughing, too. We both couldn't believe what had transpired between us from July to September and just then, in his bedroom.

As I left, he walked me to his door and said, "Let me know when you get home."

Wed 13 Sep

1:03 pm

I'm home

I wanted to text you this whole time but wanted you to focus on driving and live in the moment. But didn't want you to think I ghosted you ❤️🔥😉

❤️
You are terribly sweet and you were such a gentleman today

It felt amazing

Even in the daylight 👀

I'm SO glad we finally met 😉

I hate we waited but it was worth it

I actually like that we waited

Better words

You are so cute and I loved seeing you today

> Luv

Ooops

Actually better words for that are you are so hot

> No feelings remember?

This entire thing with you has been so hot and I've loved every bit of it

> All good
>
> How will the next chapter go

How do you want it to go?

> I want to feel this high first. Then get back to creating the next memory

I'm right there with you

END

www.ingramcontent.com/pod-product-compliance
Lightning Source LLC
Chambersburg PA
CBHW060447030426
42337CB00015B/1512